ISBN: 0615931820
ISBN-13: 978-0615931821

Library of Congress Control Number: 2014931036

Published by Tenmile Publishing LLC
Breckenridge, CO

Printed in the United States of America

Website: www.extremeautumn.com
Author Website: garrettfisher.me

All photos in this book are available as prints, digital files, and framed prints. Please visit the book website to order.

Extreme Autumn:
Fall in Colorado

Extreme Autumn?   6

The Meaning of Autumn   8

Hints   10

Perspective   12

Immersion   15

Defiance   24

Mixed Signals   26

The Rugged & The Sanguine   28

Peak   43

Night   48

Water   51

The Esoteric   54

Aerial   56

Last Gasp   66

It's Over   73

Black and White   75

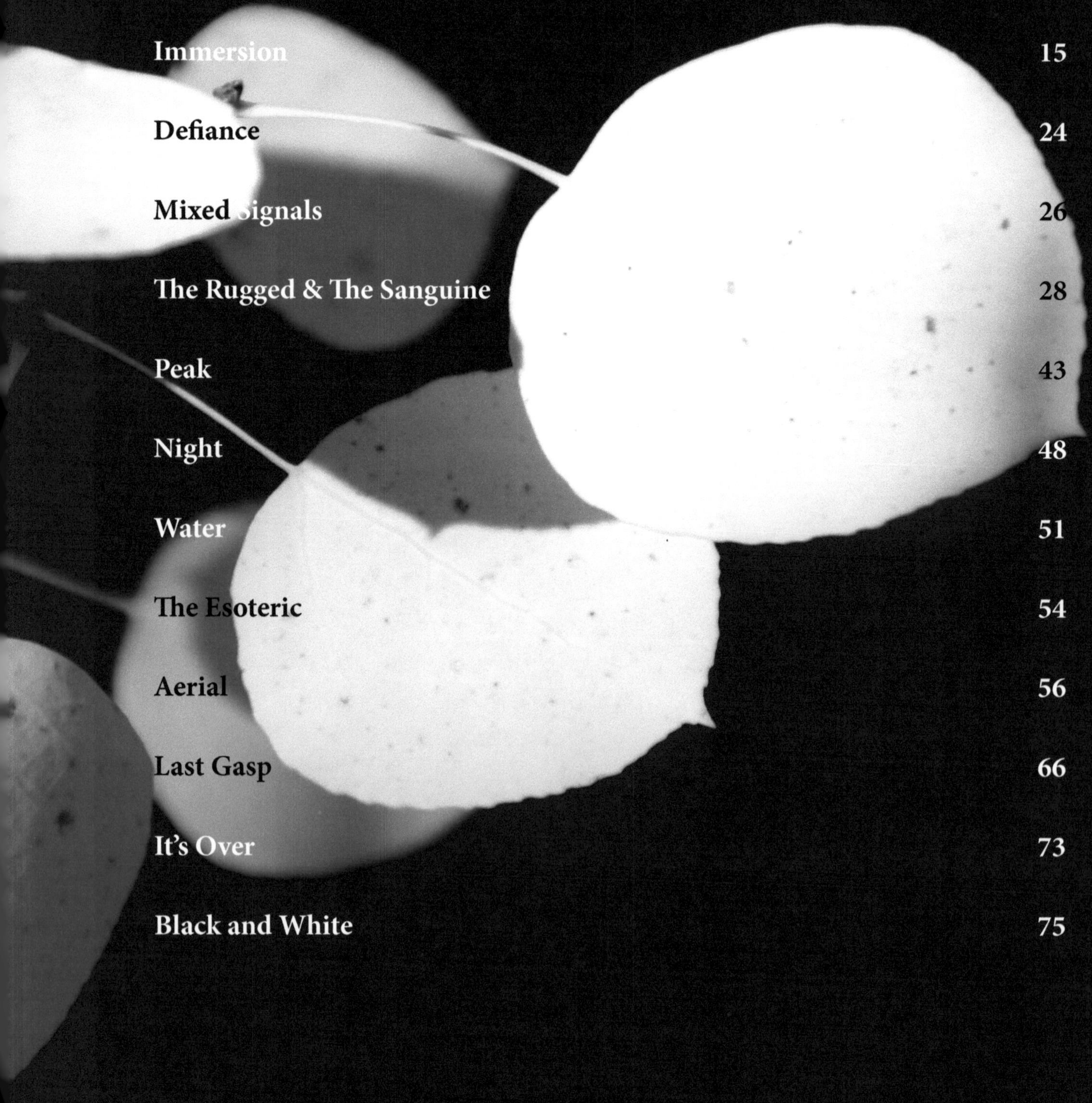

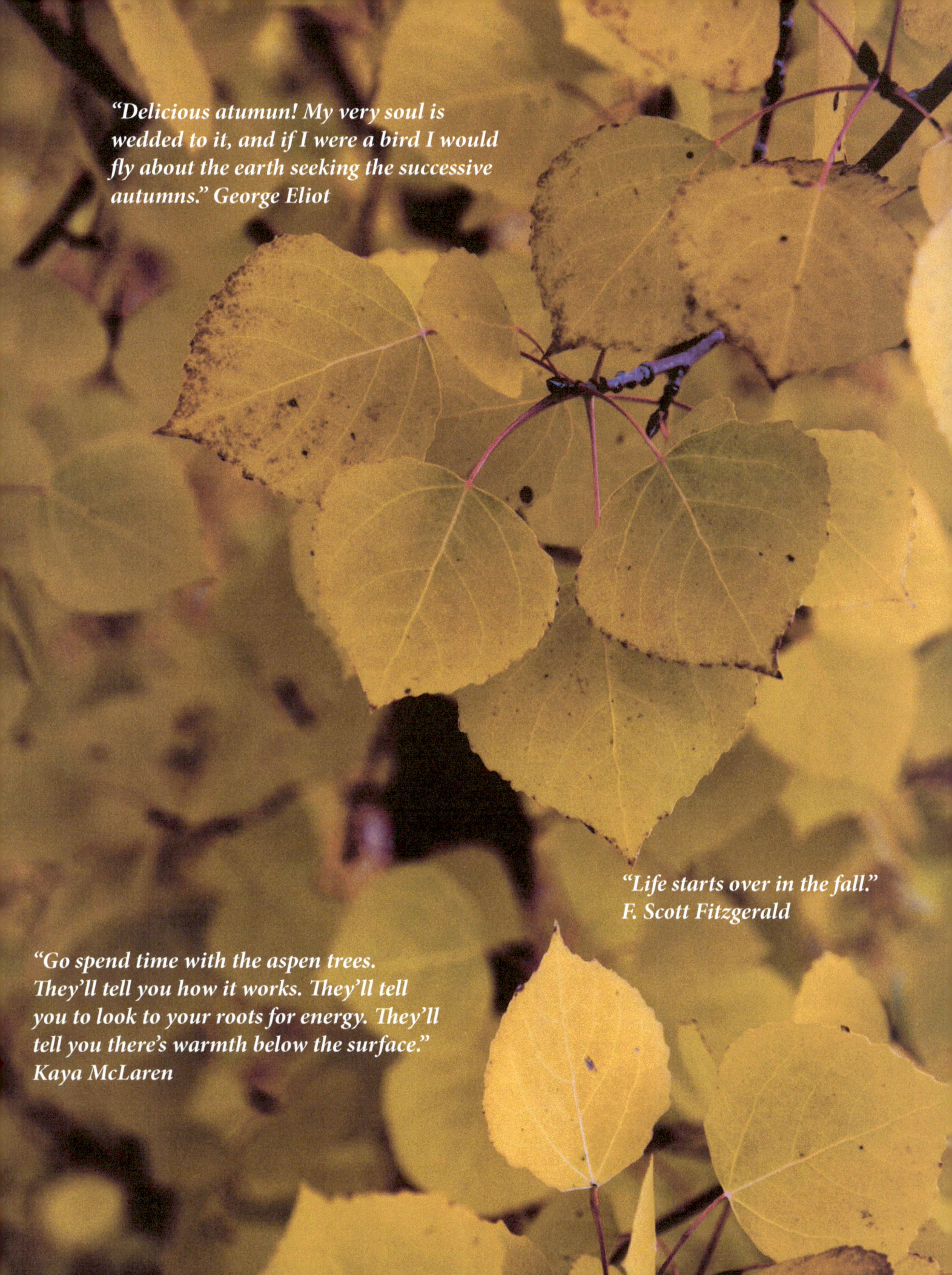

"Delicious atumun! My very soul is wedded to it, and if I were a bird I would fly about the earth seeking the successive autumns." George Eliot

"Life starts over in the fall." F. Scott Fitzgerald

"Go spend time with the aspen trees. They'll tell you how it works. They'll tell you to look to your roots for energy. They'll tell you there's warmth below the surface." Kaya McLaren

Extreme Autumn?

What about autumn could possibly be extreme? Autumnal photography has to be one of the most tranquil and serene genres of art – something that belongs on a brochure for preplanning one's burial – scenes worthy of the deepest contemplation of the meaning of life and the existence of the universe. You know, the typical red leaf floating in a pond…….

That is all well and good in most places on the planet. Fall comes in progressively….. with the standard drivel about the "burst of autumn color." Let us be realistic. Fall can be nasty. Windy. Rainy. Downright ugly. In fact, mental health professionals will tell you that autumn has the highest incidence rate of mental health issues out of all of the seasons. That only makes sense – as in the Americas our creepiest holiday falls at the tail end of the leaf season – one bent on spookiness and fear and capitalizing on the apparent evils of pumpkins and swirling fallen leaves in the wind. The reality is – few people photo bad weather in autumn – because it's ugly. At best, a contemplative red maple in the fog is worthy of a photo. A rainy and windy day? People hide.

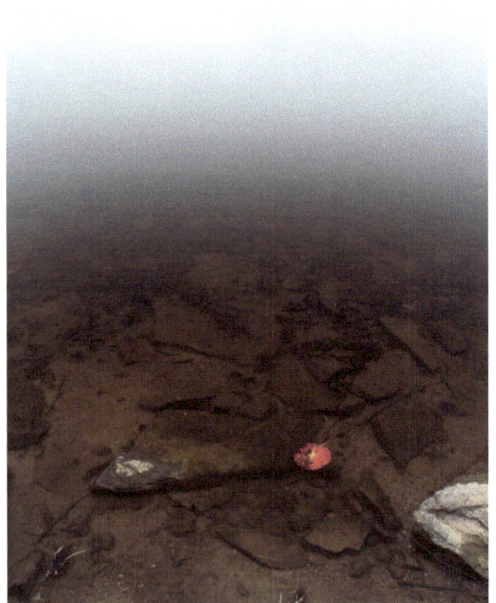

Typical Red Leaf Floating in Pond

Colorado is different – especially in the high country. We don't really get autumn rain of any consequence in the high country near 10,000 feet. Its either snow, blue skies, or wind. Wind would tear the beauty right off the trees in most places. Here, the trees expect it and are hardened. The net result is we get an odd amalgam of extreme weather – schizophrenic renditions of summer, fall, and winter all in the same week in September – followed by pleasant blue sky bliss. Angry snow storms that first strike at 11,000 feet spare the trees entirely at 9,000 feet – so in the same town, it is possible to see the expiration of fall replete with brown, dead leaves on the ground and yet descend a bit and the leaves are green with color in the middle.

For most locales, autumn leaves with snow on them are almost impossible – first due to the need for extreme cold and snow early in the season – and secondly because the trees drop their leaves due to the weight of the snow. Here the leaves only drop two days after getting frozen; otherwise, they hold the weight of the snow quite well. To add to the unusualness, the high peaks often have decent snow above the timberline, adding epic beauty as a backdrop. To make things even more atypical, deciduous trees are a minority in Colorado. Aspens are the dominant species that puts on color with a handful of other species showing up here and there – and these other species especially along riverbanks at lower altitudes. So a person can literally go from a snow-capped peak, descend through Engelmann spruce pines, lodge pole pines, dry desert-like sagebrush and then a fertile riverbank with stands of colorful trees – all with aspens interspersed in connected groves between 6,000 feet and 12,000 feet elevation. Color here is like an artist's paintbrush – explosive accents painted here and there among wild terrain and ecosystem variety. Add an airplane, 14,000 foot peaks, and passive-aggressive weather and autumn like few have ever seen it becomes possible to enjoy – while sitting in your underwear drinking hot chocolate.

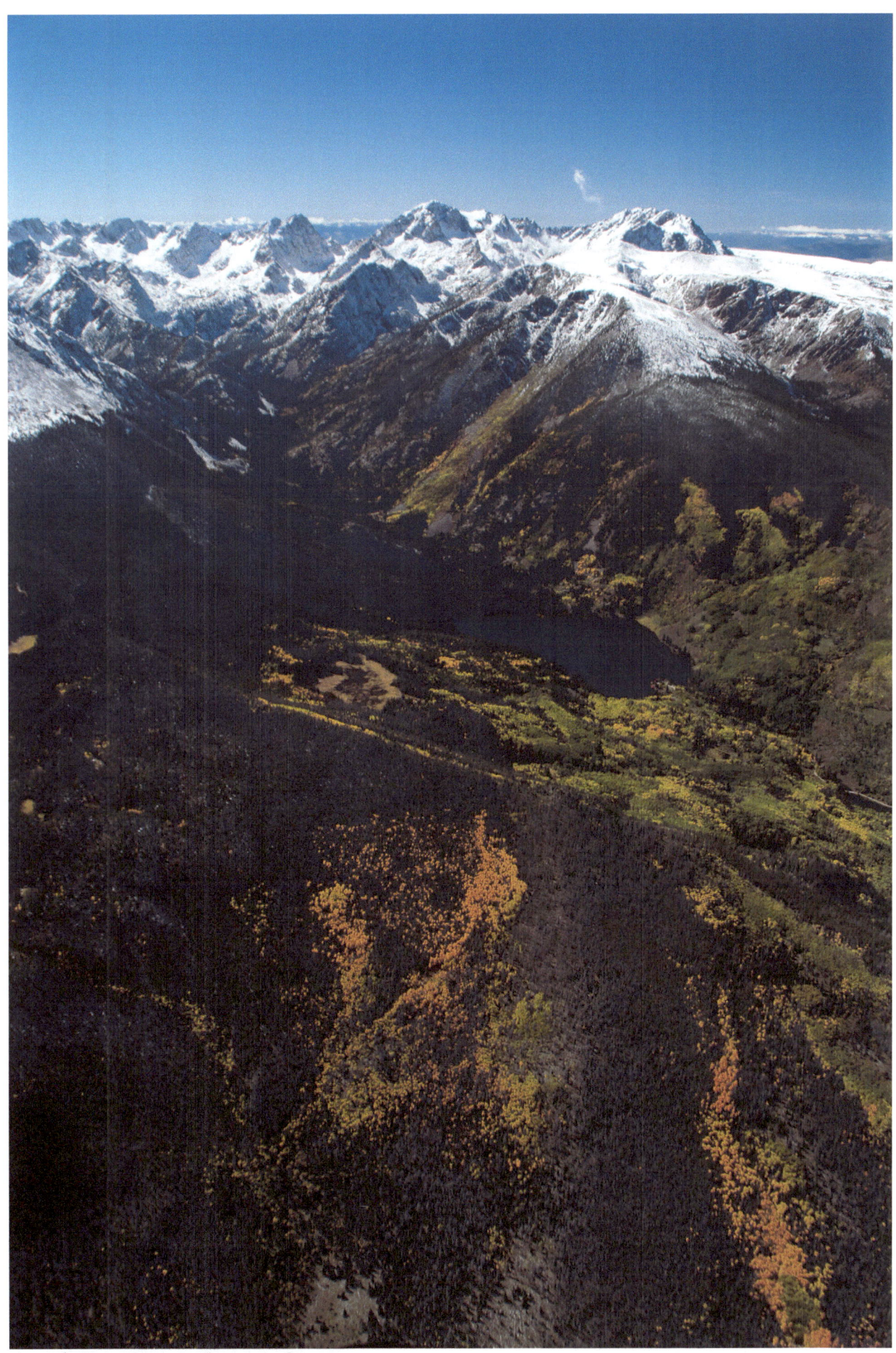

Aerial, Gore Range - Summit County

The Meaning of Autumn

I will simplistically state that fall is my favorite season – without question – and has remained so while living in CO, NY, and NC. I am one of those rare persons that hate summer. When evaluating the list of changes that takes place when summer comes: weather, plants, animals, air quality, human habits – there are only two benefits: long days and leaves on trees. The rest is a liability. Fall is the antidote to the horrors of summer.

Growing up in upstate NY, there were few who hated summer. Winters were painfully difficult to live through for a variety of reasons – the primary being the fact that parts of the Buffalo metro area had less sun than Seattle in the middle of winter. Couple that with short days and the fact that Buffalo often got mid-winter rain and mud, and there was next to no reason to live there for that part of the year. When summer came, everything went opposite. Days were long, sunshine incredibly abundant, and temperatures warm to hot. What naturally follows was mind-numbing.

Western New Yorkers would reach manic levels of hysteria – running from picnics to family reunions to events laden with nasty beer consumed by profligate and very cold poolsides and starting all over again. For a two-month period, the pace of life was an unsustainable silliness that would wear out anyone with an introverted, contemplative side that needed to be left alone. To make matters worse, outdoor activities were plagued with mosquitos – and in my case, the shores of Lake Erie and area waterfalls turned into an algae-infused mucky cesspit. Flow rates lowered, water stagnated, waves disappeared on the Lake, and crowds of inebriates showed up, smoked pot, drank beer, and littered.

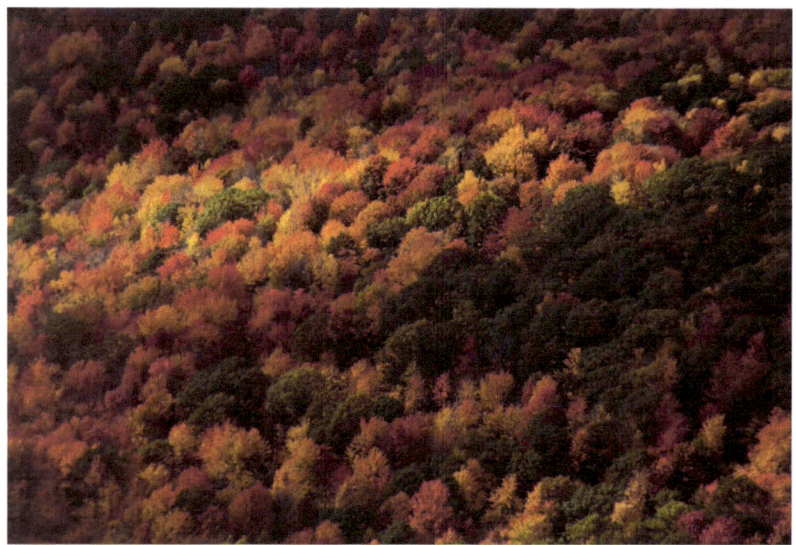

Evening Flight in the Cub - Upstate New York, October

When the first cold front roared out of Canada (usually late August to early September), it set a number of wonderful things in motion. Algae died off. Mosquitoes expired. Persistent summer haze (read: wallowing in pre-combusted air and airborne human particulates) blew "away." Pools were closed at Labor Day. Children returned to state educational penitentiaries. Outdoor faux socializing ended. And even more significant: football season started. What once happened outdoors in a crowded mass retreated to reclining chairs, television watching, card tables, and basements. For some reason, people in WNY seemed to love the pride of a finished basement and to spend inordinate amounts of time underground avoiding what remaining miniscule solar energy might harm them. With the people and microbial infestation removed, then the beauty started.

Fall ushers in a rapidly enlivening period of wonderful weather and scenery. Leaves begin their initial change. Temperatures drop at night. Bonfire season kicks in – as does apple cider season. For me, the best flying of the year happened in the fall – and I would take tons of flights in the Cub on a calm, chilly evening with the hillsides filled with color and some of the calmest, most beautiful air to fly in. The first real wind events would start – an energizing warm wind out of the south would usher in a glorious smell – one I later learned after moving to the Southeast was the pine trees in the southern part of the country. Waves showed up at the Lake again. Algae died off in the river systems – and any lingering August droughts were certain to disappear with lake-induced rains. For me, life resumed after a summer hiatus. For everyone else, it was time to fatten up for winter hibernation.

I had a dream once when I was in my late teens. In the dream, I am not sure if I had died, or if simply humans had finally made it to peace. What I mean is personal to everyone – some call it heaven, others paradise, others Nirvana. Whatever your rendition is, it was paradise to me – and in the dream, there was a calmness and joy that could be wrapped into a blanket and worn. Humans had finally achieved peace and bliss – nothing but joy in this dream. It was unlike anything I had dreamed about before nor have since. The particularly interesting facet was my surroundings in this paradise. I was standing near the property I grew up on: a place with forests, open fields, views, ponds, and the grass airstrip. The sky was the deepest blue possible. The trees were the brightest full peak of color imaginable – a scene to this day I can remember from a dream well over a decade ago. To top it all off, there was a double rainbow. My version of paradise is the most resplendent fall day possible.

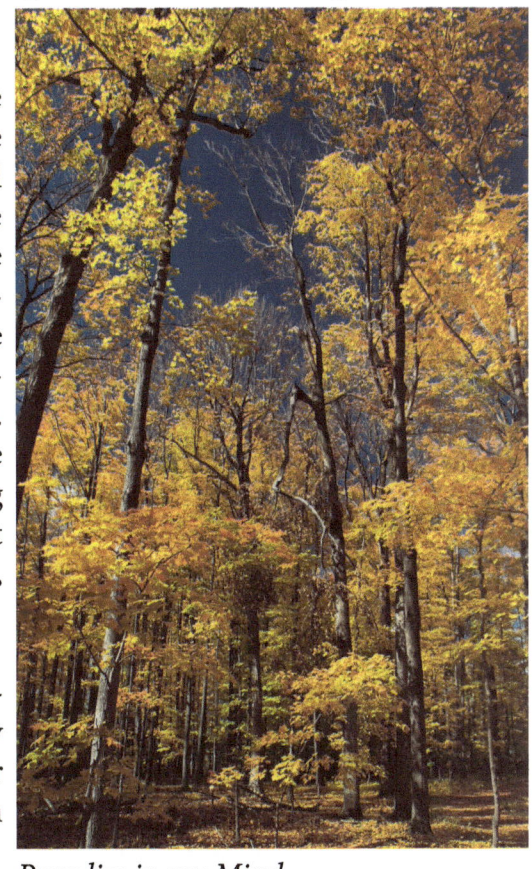

Paradise in my Mind

I had an opportunity to experience a version of this scenario while working taking photos of the fall colors here in the Rockies. On one particular afternoon (one of many), the air was dry, the sky a crystal deep blue, no wind, and temperatures in the mid 60s. The colors in the particular area I was in were at full peak – with incredible views of the Tenmile Range and blue sky all at the same time. This particular section was rather open – so it was safe enough to listen to music in the headphones – something I generally avoid deep in the mountain forests alone due to many large predator species that enjoy the leaves too. I was listening to Beethoven's Symphony No. 5 – and for the first time that I can remember (while awake), time stopped. I remember saying that it "felt like I lived forever for an hour;" the joy and contentment transcended all verticals of thought – and nothing else mattered. Well, until the sun went behind Peak 1 and that was the end of that.

This book is my expression of what I consider to be pure joy, epic beauty, the stoppage of time, peace, and paradise. A manifestation of many years of desire, this is the culmination of what I have wanted to do for over a decade: make time stop and photo the autumn relentlessly from start to finish.

The project, although a lifelong desire, simply landed in my lap. I had no expectation of chasing the autumn this year; rather, I had no clue what to expect and was working on another book and photography project. Being our first year out West, I knew that aspens turned color – I didn't know when, how intense, how long, and where. One particular day, about 1% of the aspens had started to change color in mid-September and I spent some time figuring them out and finding the best artistic angle. Two days later, my wife and I drove to Kenosha Pass in pursuit of what I had read would be an epic explosion of color. We got there – able to enjoy resplendent green aspens – no color. On the way back, we took a random turn down a forest service road in our front wheel drive car with no knowledge of what we would see – only the hope that we would land back in Breckenridge. The road was Boreas Pass Rd on the Park County side. As we ascended into the backcountry after sunset, colors were nearly explosive. Reds and oranges were present amongst the aspen groves – something I did not know was possible. As we descended on the Breckenridge side, the trees were in full peak. I returned that night at 11PM to catch them in full moon color. Following that adventure, a month long mania ensued – hiking, climbing, off-roading, driving, and flying at every single hour possible – morning to night, all weekend long, during rain, sun, snow, and wind – chasing the progression of fall from the timberline down the river valleys until the last leaf fell. It is with tremendous pleasure that I present an extreme autumn, Rocky Mountain style, from 7890' elevation to 14,000'.

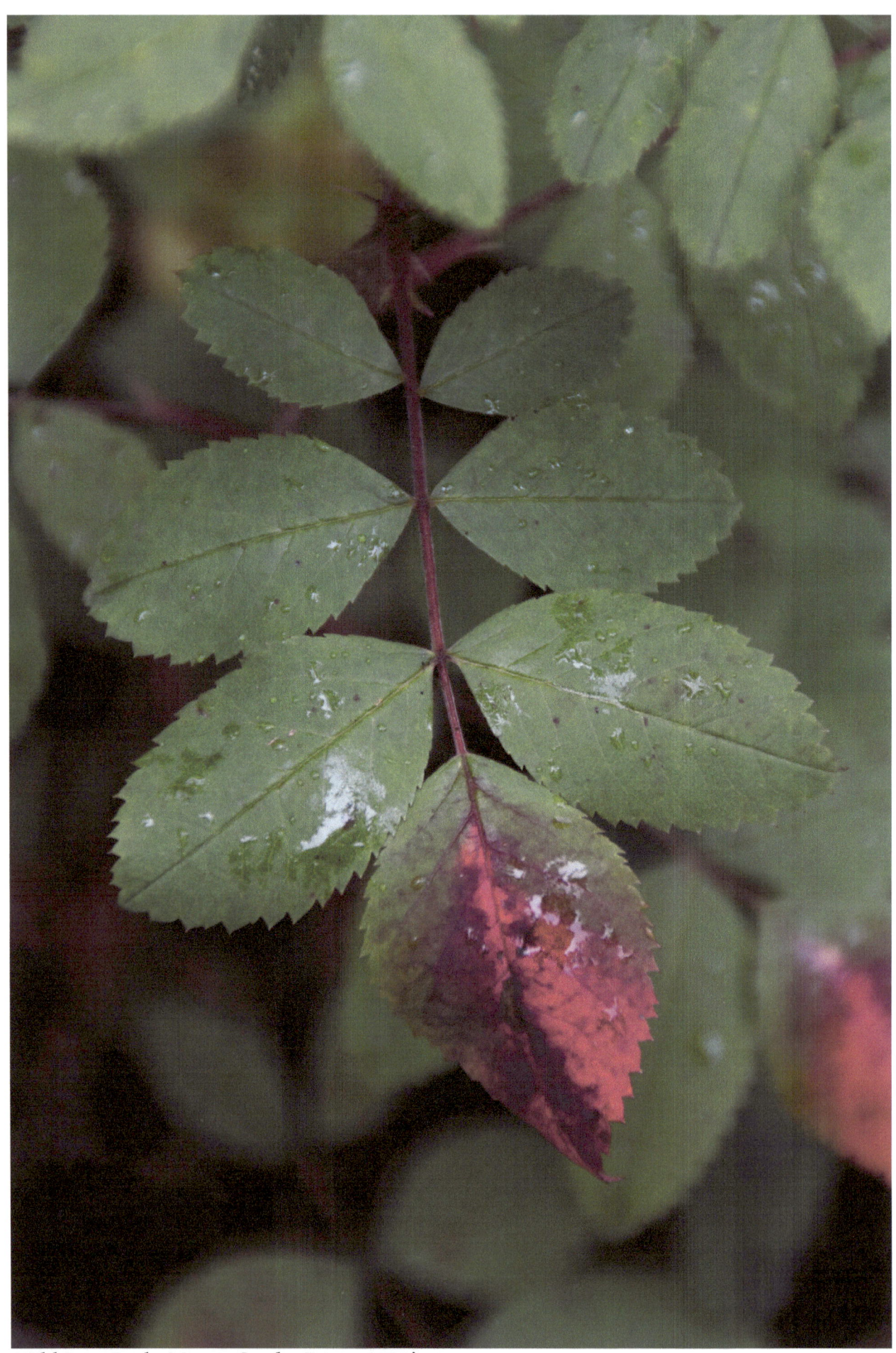

Wild Rose Bush, Miners Creek - Frisco, 9780'

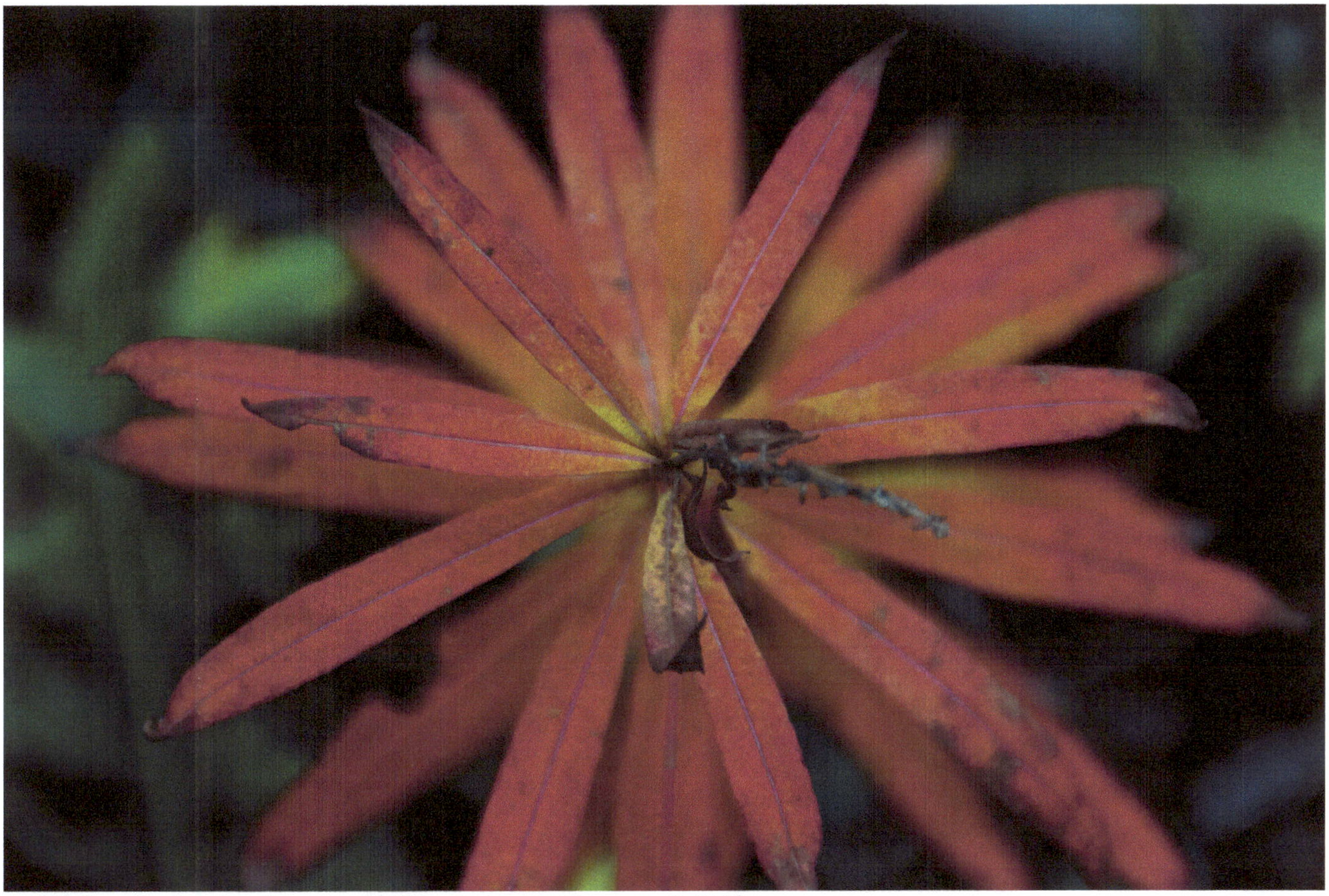

![Underbrush photo]

Underbrush, Lower Cataract Lake - Summit County, 8,640'

Autumn gives a few hints well in advance that it is coming. In Colorado, those subtleties manifest themselves in lush undergrowth that appears in various moist locations. In this particular area near Lower Cataract Falls (above), the terrain is north-facing and near a waterfall (below) and river system that fans out in multiple directions. It is so moist that there are plants hanging from some of the tree branches in the shade – things I have personally only seen in the Pacific Northwest and the lower flanks of the Andes mountains in the tropics. In this moist undergrowth, plants give warning to the coming change in early September.

There is a cornucopia of species – and they all show varying levels of color. Bright red rose hips, yellow, orange, and red tinted leaves – part green, part full color. Bushes and scrubs also begin their changes well in advance of trees. In this particular photo, an herbaceous plant has already changed its color – after a brief life of slightly over 3 and a half months. Only 25 days later and we revisited the site – and it was snow covered. By next June, the snow will be gone and the undergrowth resuming it's short burst of activity.

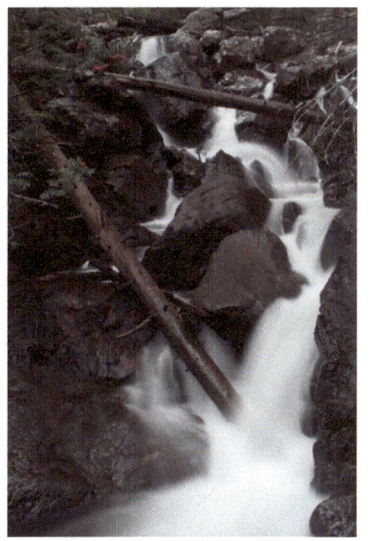

A wild rose bush gives a subtle early warning of the presence of fall (left). Nestled along Miner's Creek in Frisco, this site is a favorite of mine for outdoor writing in the summer – a resplendent alpine stream with towering spruce trees and groves of lodge pole pines. In late August, the undergrowth mixes summer green with near explosive colors – what most would consider weeds were a display of what was to come. The surrealism of the site lay in the fact that it was summer in every other respect – temperature, sunshine, afternoon thunderstorms, and abundant green. Having experienced a (relatively speaking) warm summer, there were many days without a frost, so no particular element other than the turning pages of the calendar brought these colors to fruition.

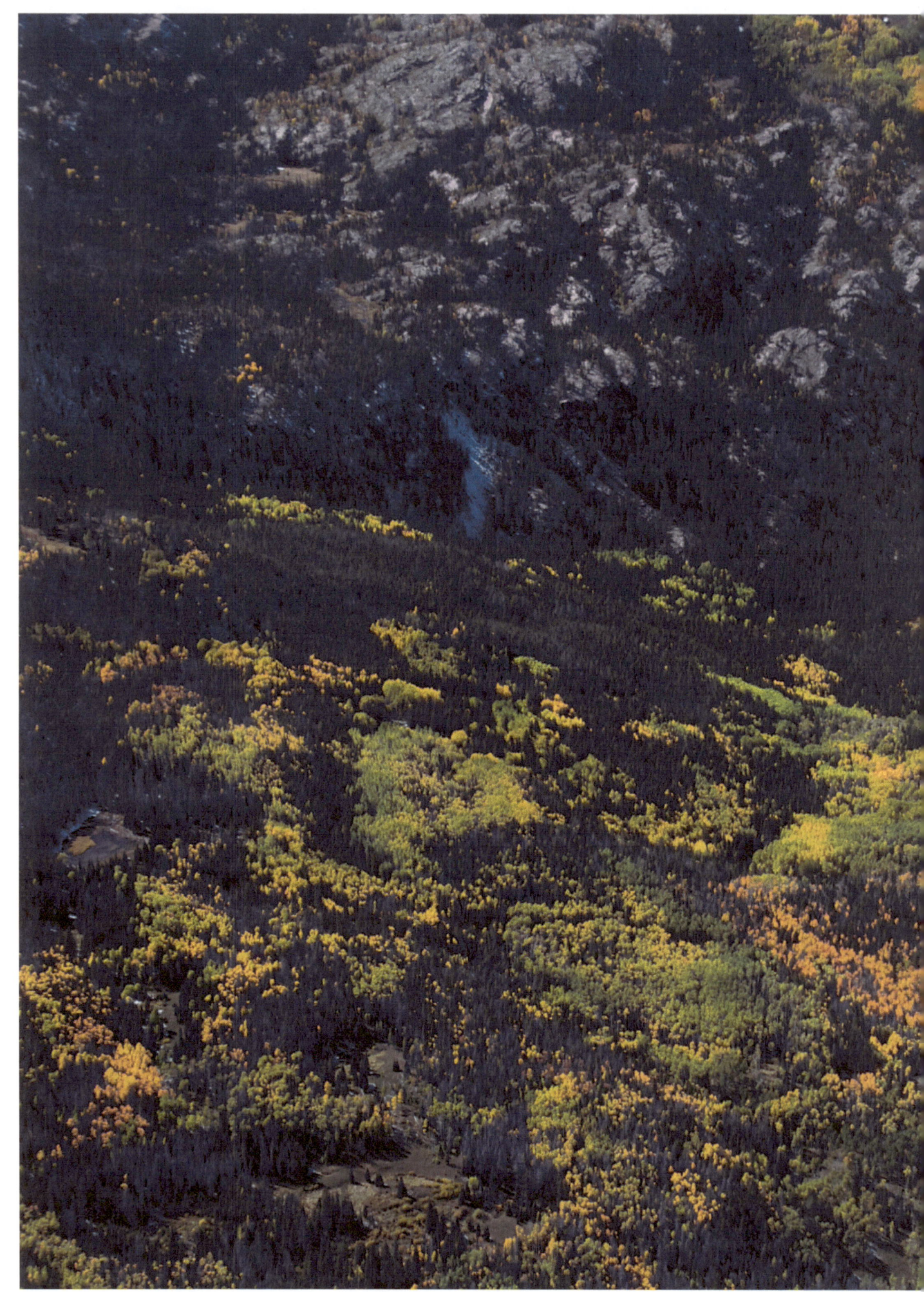

Lower Cataract Lake, Summit County, 8,620'

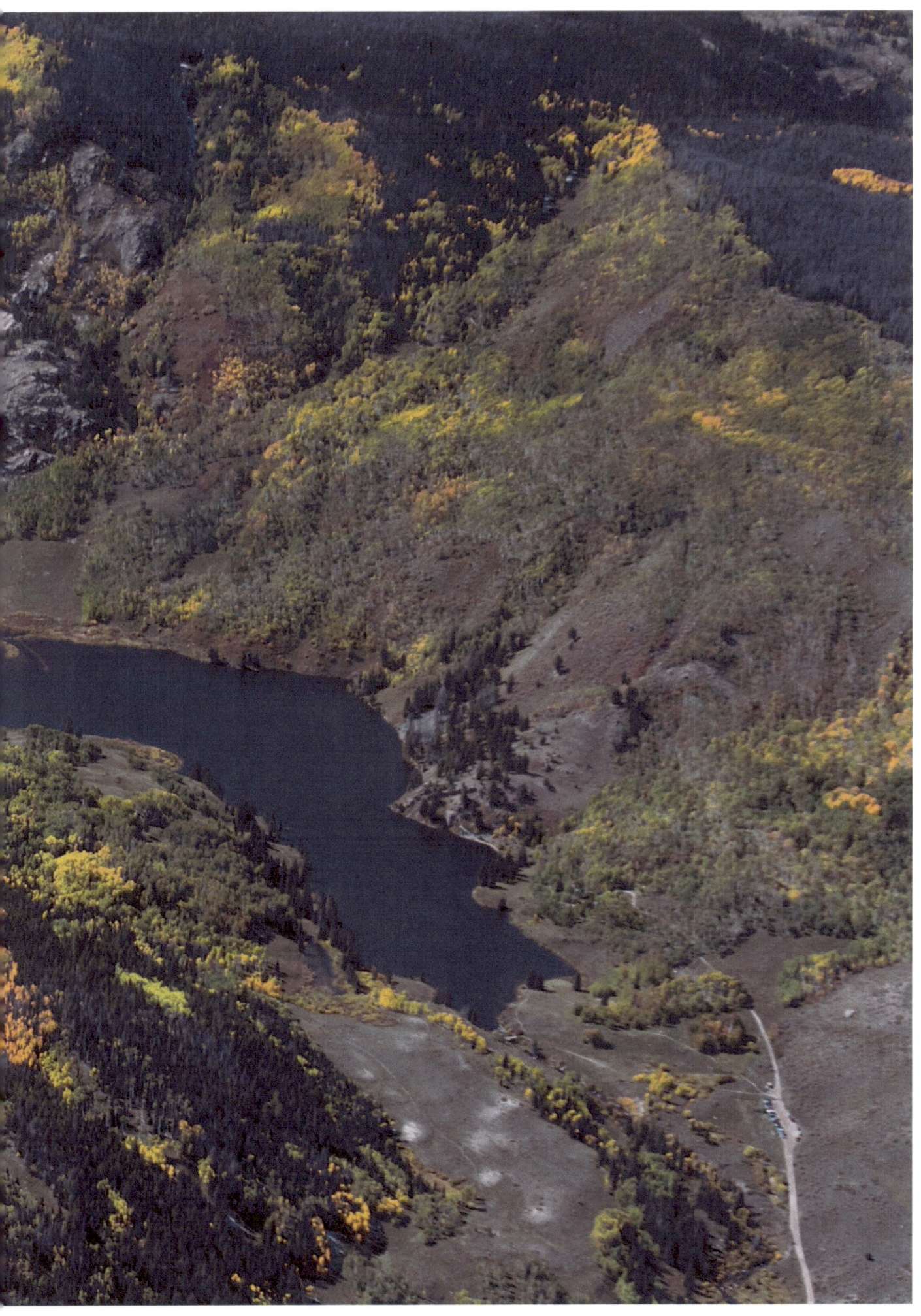

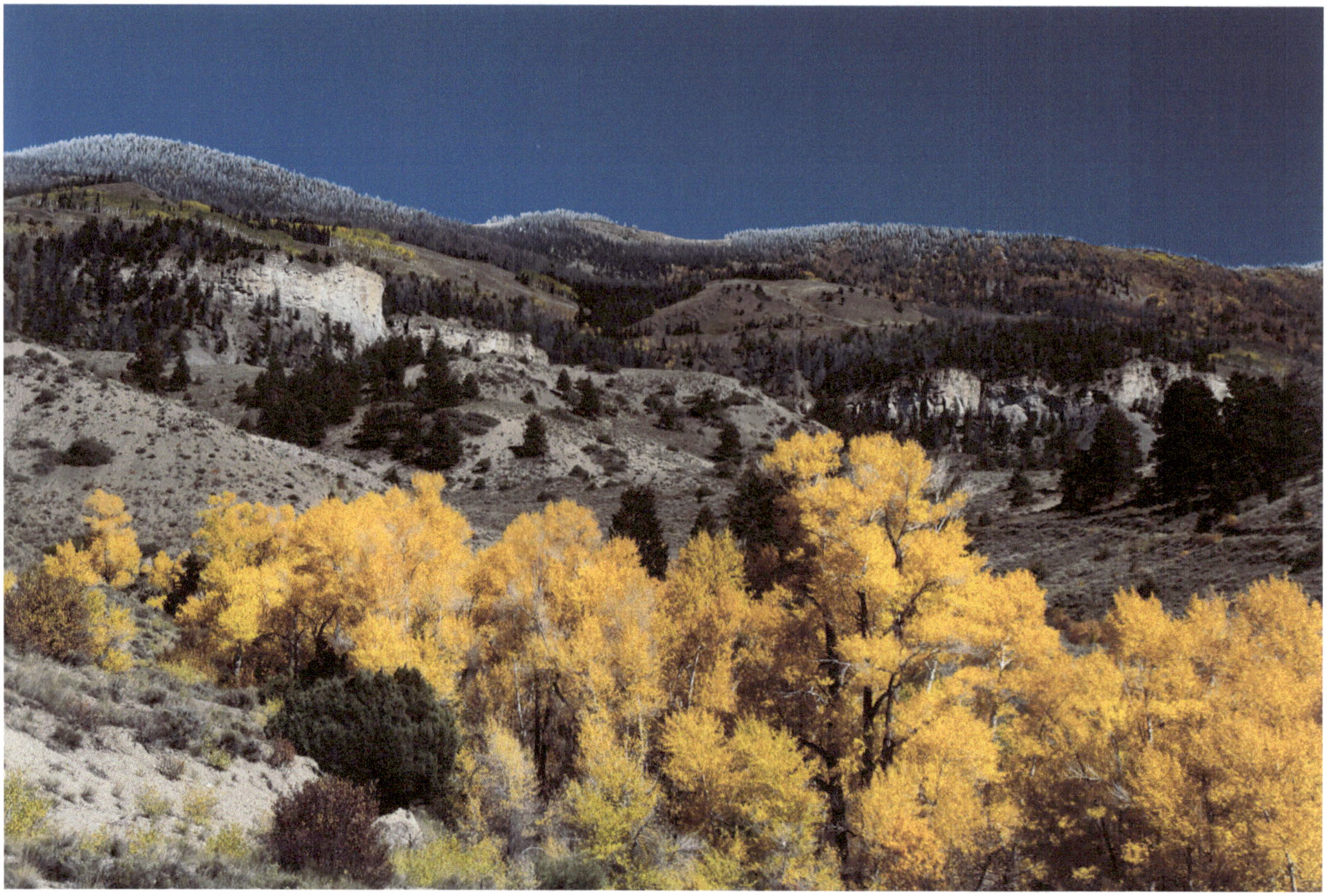

Cottonwoods with Williams Peak Range in Background, Summit County, 8,020'

(Above) An excellent example of the worlds of difference in a short distance as elevation changes. At the base of this photo, elevation is 8020' in the northern part of Summit County – region that is practically a desert. The only reason the trees are alive is a small mountain stream coming off the peaks in the background. As the terrain ascends, juniper bushes give way to sparse pine trees followed by aspens, lodge poles, and finally spruce trees. On this particular late September day, light snowfall and rime ice is gracing the highest part of the peaks, which culminate over 11,000 feet in elevation. Interestingly, in this part of Colorado, eight thousand feet is nearly a desert. In other sections of the state, much lower elevations are even more moist. In this region, the dryness is due to a rain shadow from a north-south mountain range that runs from the Wyoming border all the way into the highest section of the state.

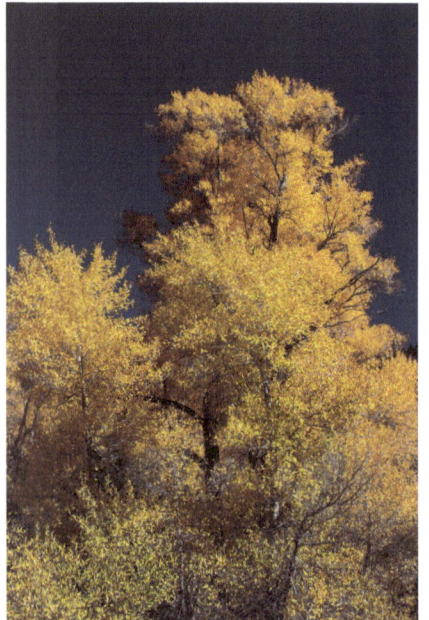

There is a particular surrealism undergoing the transition from viewing the grove of cottonwoods to actually stepping in amongst them. From the outside, strong Colorado sun hits the parched soil – and although the day was fresh and cool, there is a desert-style heat emanating from the ground. I actually felt sympathy for what small, sad plants could manage to eke out an existence amongst the herbaceous crucible. Entering the grove of cottonwoods is akin to a resurrection – the quiet gurgle of a pittance of a stream, grasses, non-desert pines and explosive color on all sides and above. With the backdrop of rich, deep blue, it was an oasis of color, life, and natural art.

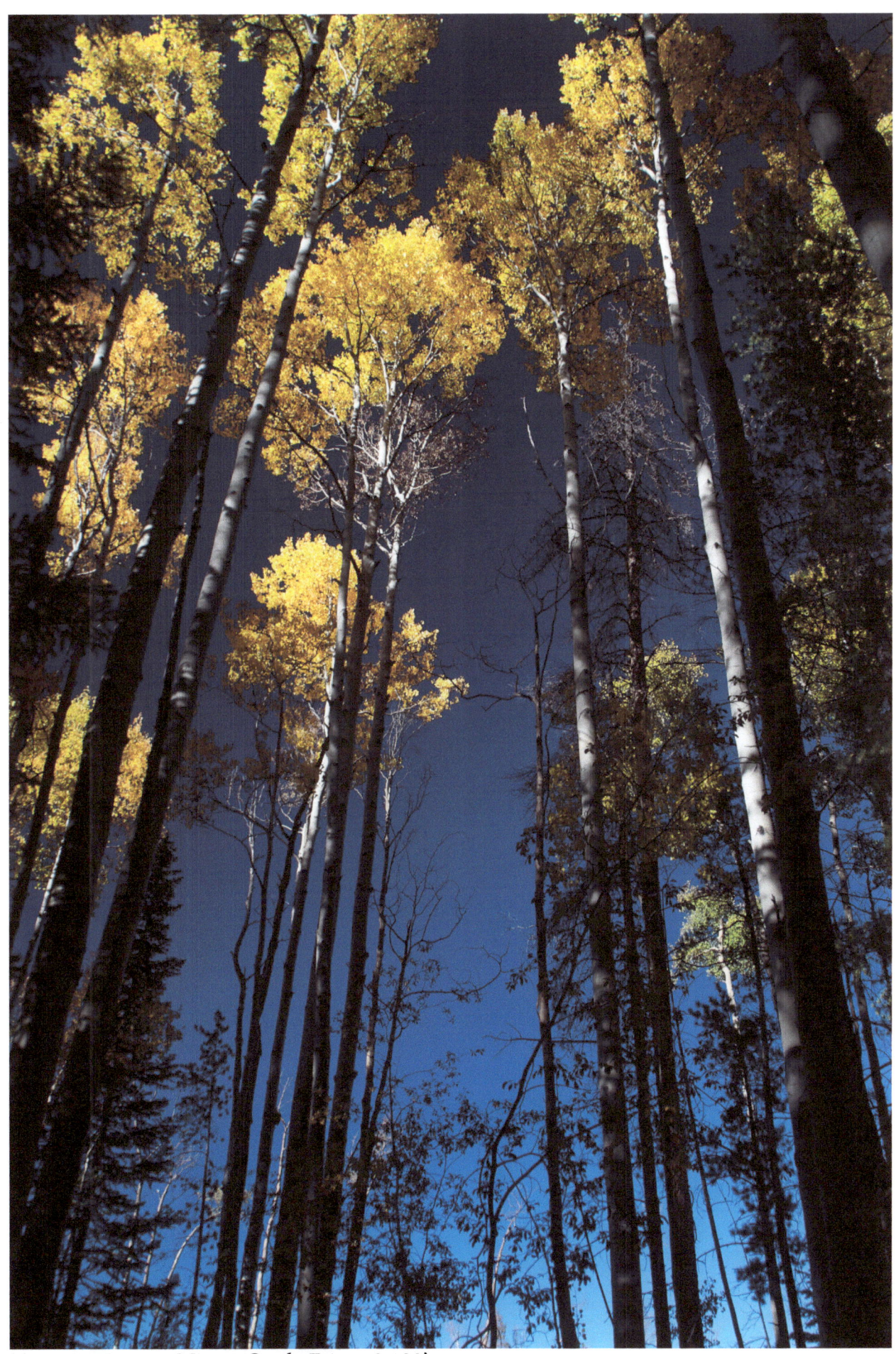

Towering Aspens, Miners Creek, Frisco, 9,180'

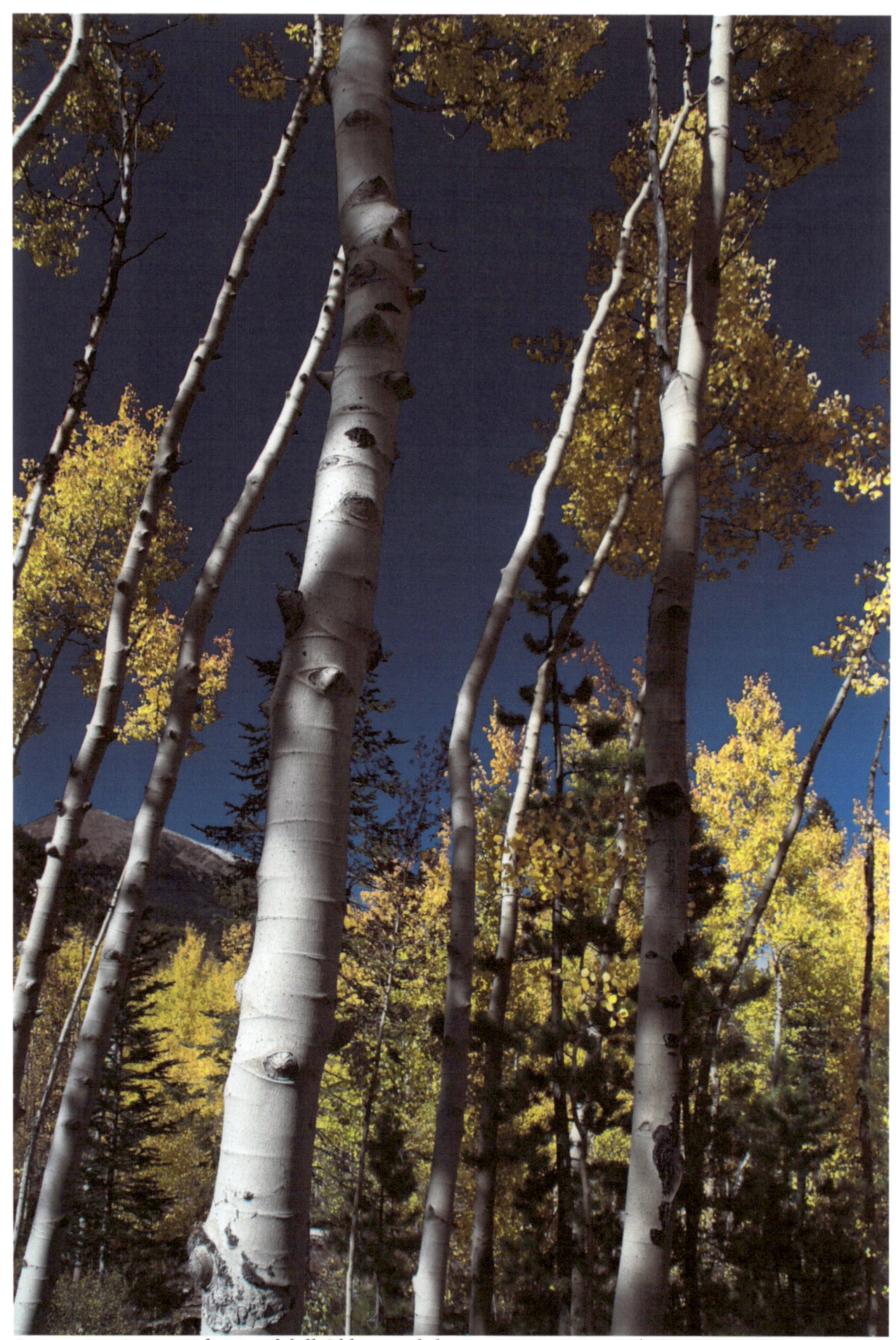

Remaining Aspens After Beetlekill Obliterated the Forest, Frisco, 9,120'

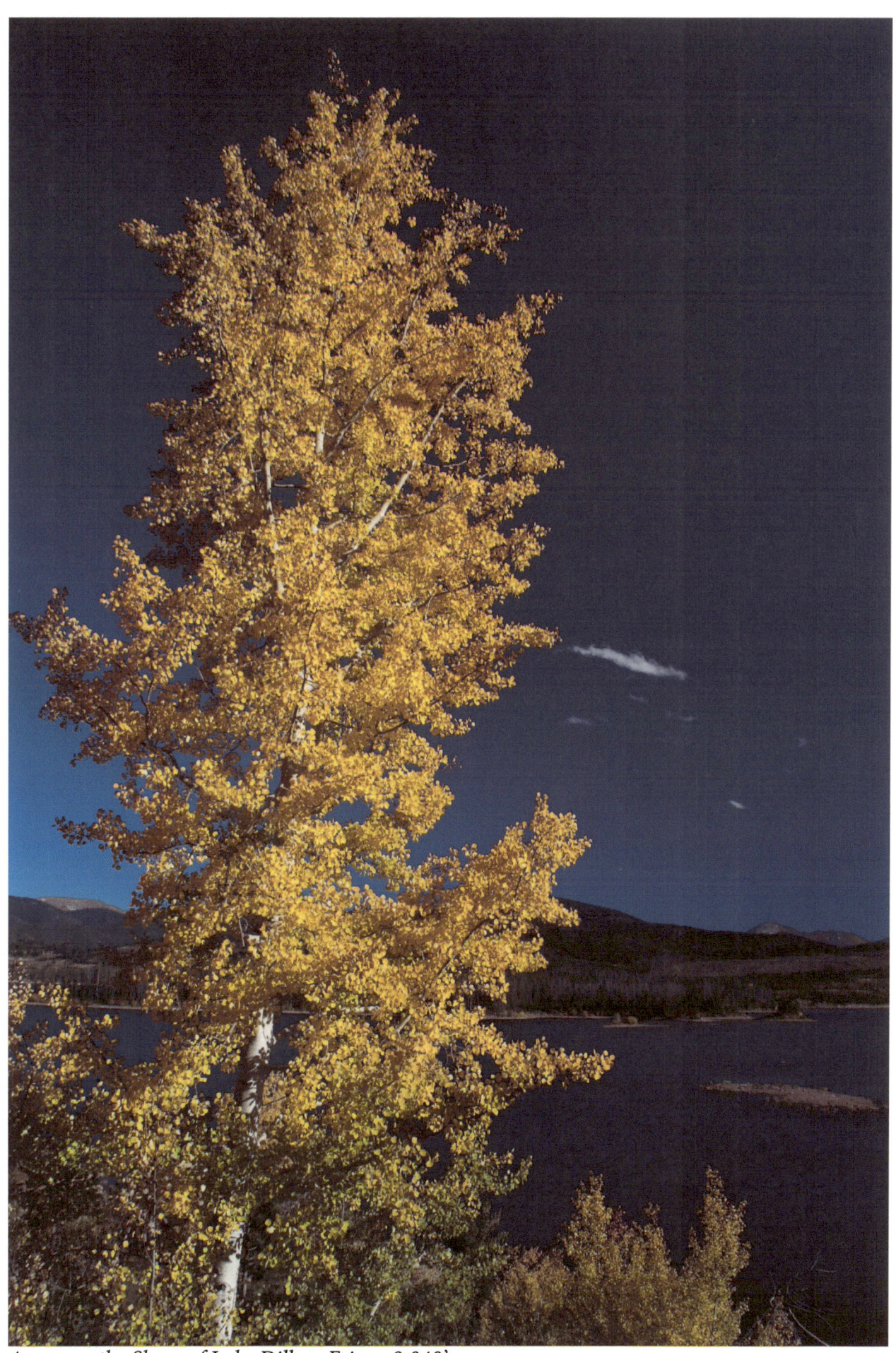

Aspen on the Shore of Lake Dillon, Frisco, 9,040'

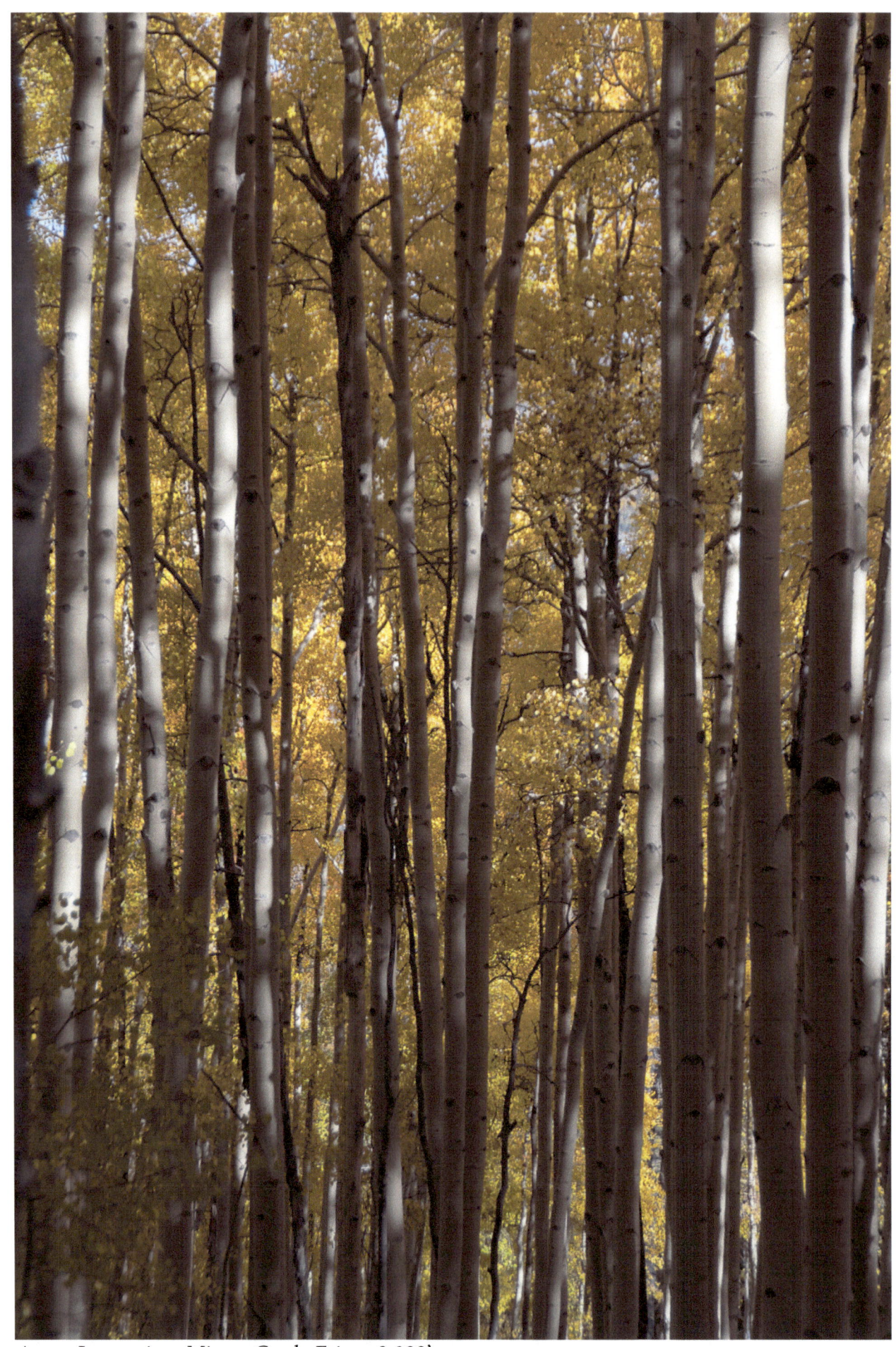

Aspen Immersion, Miners Creek, Frisco, 9,320'

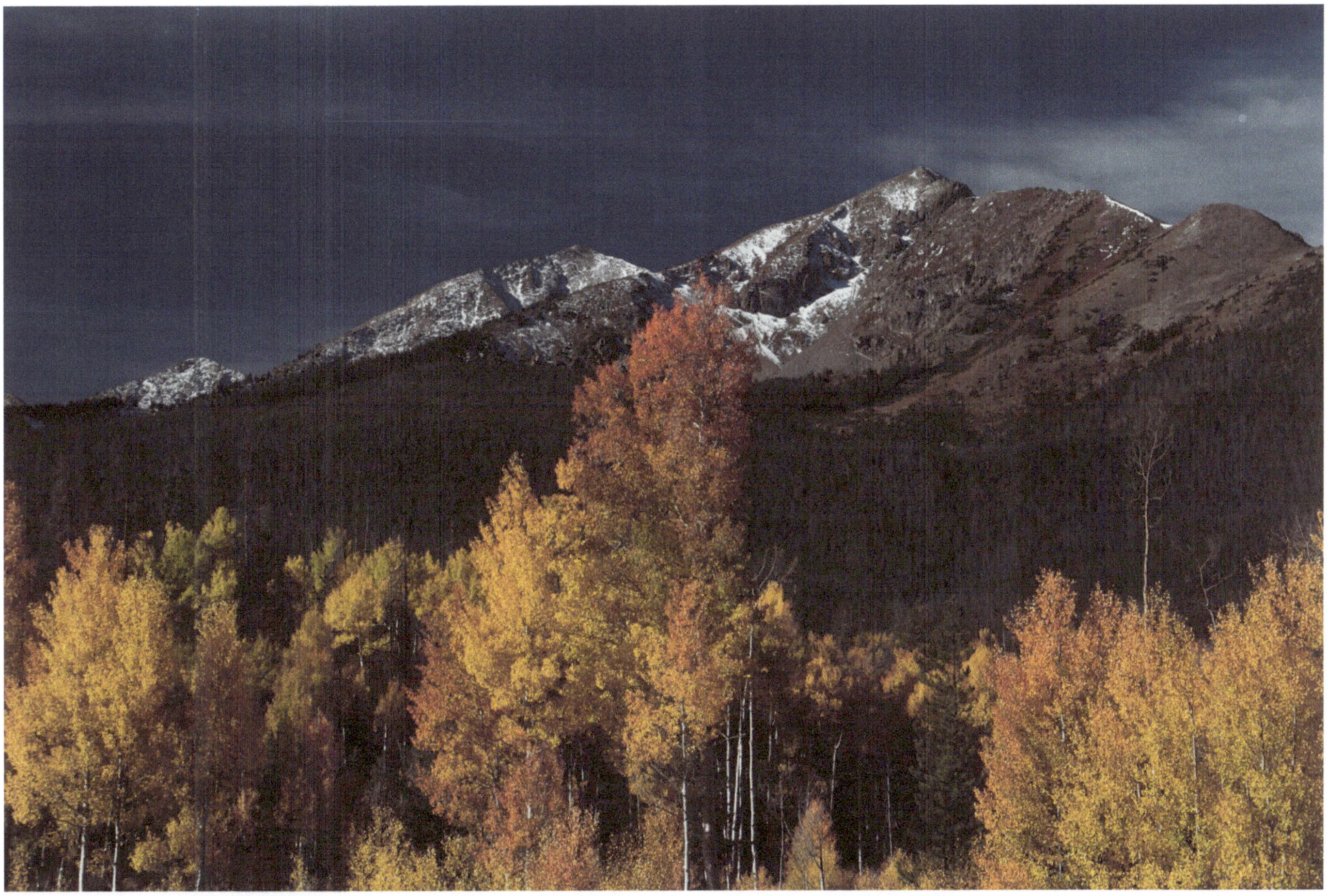

Peak 1, Frisco, 9,160'

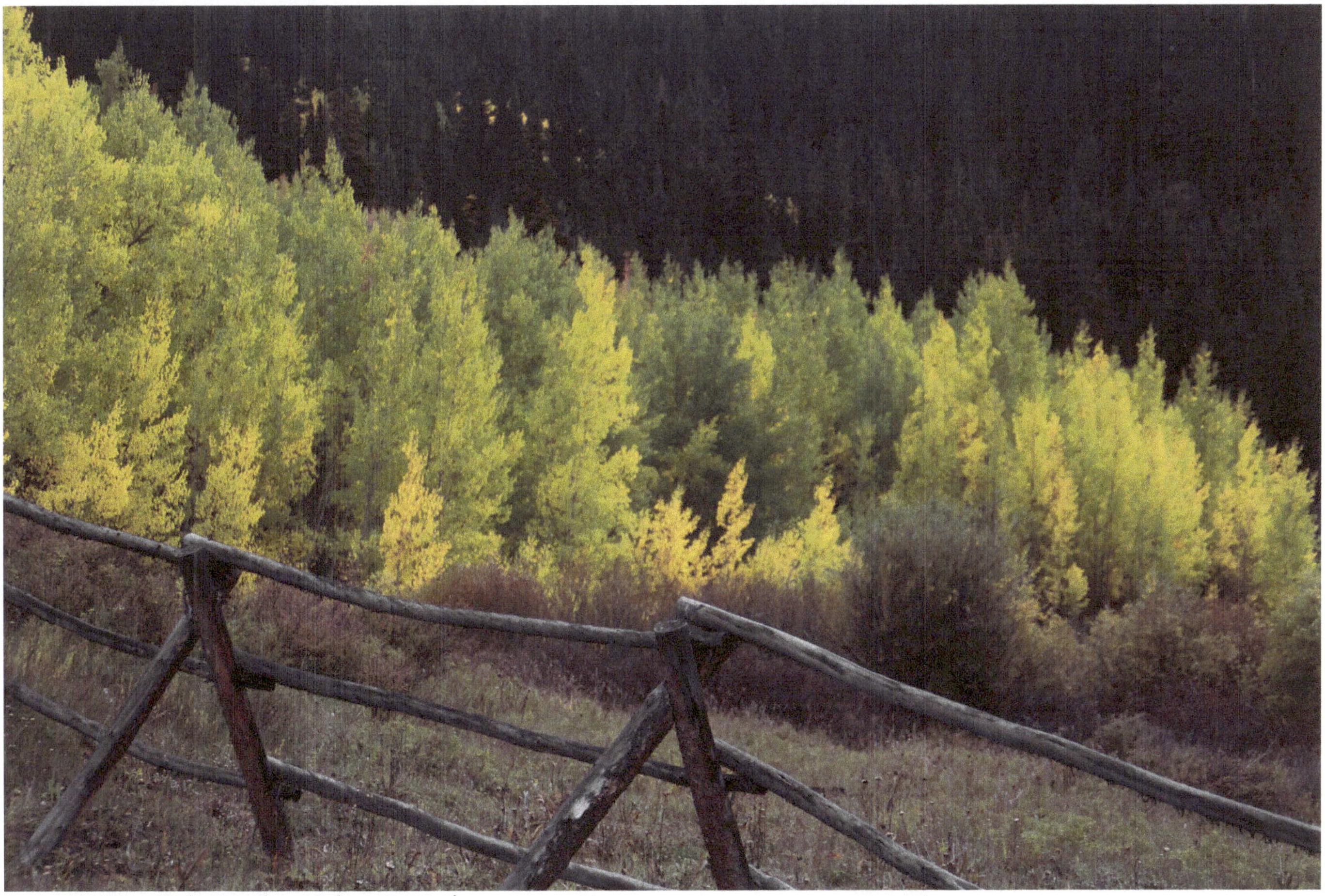

Boreas Pass Rd, Breckenridge, 9,910'

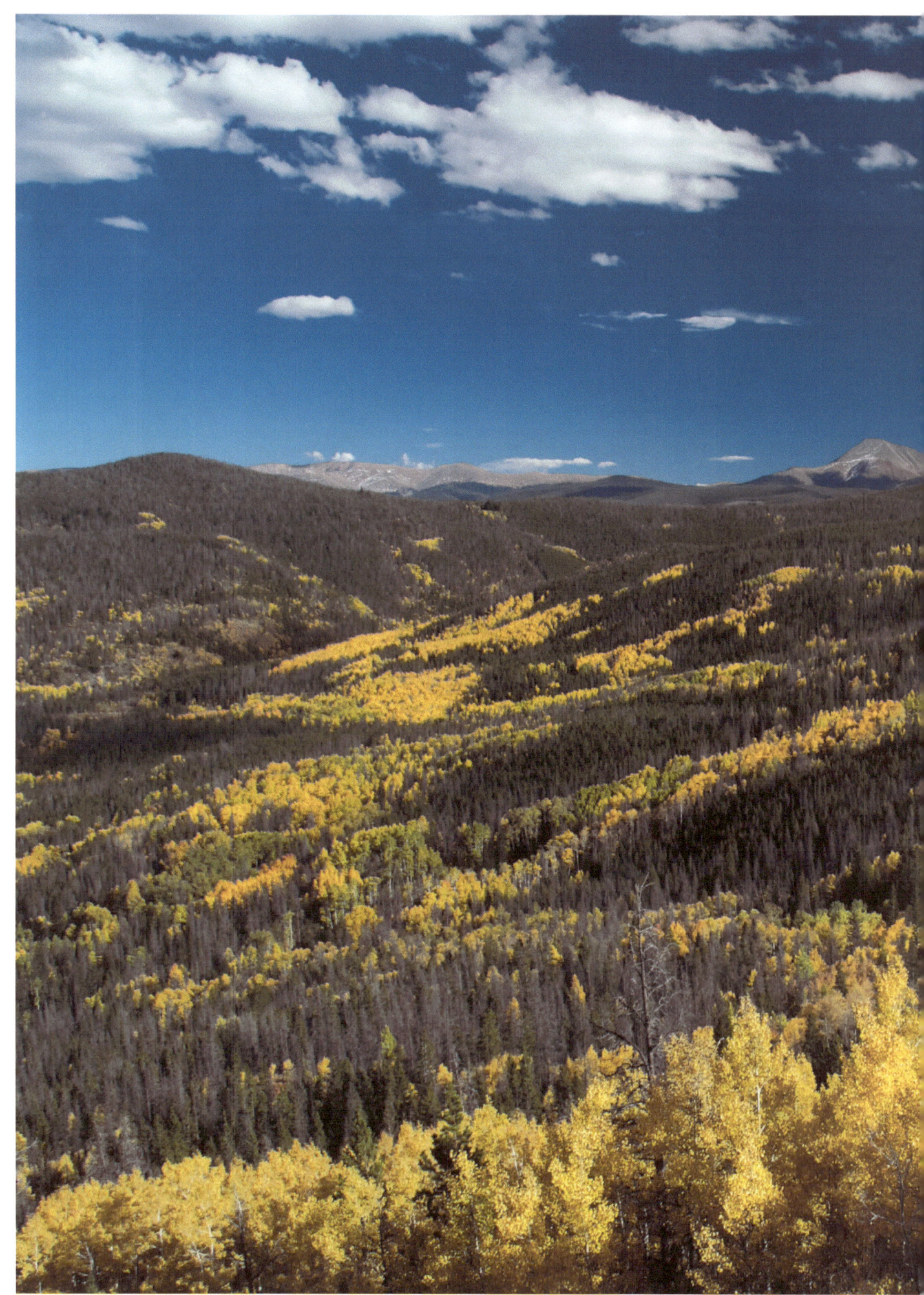

Trail to Mt. Royal (Mt. Baldy in Background), Frisco, 9,800'

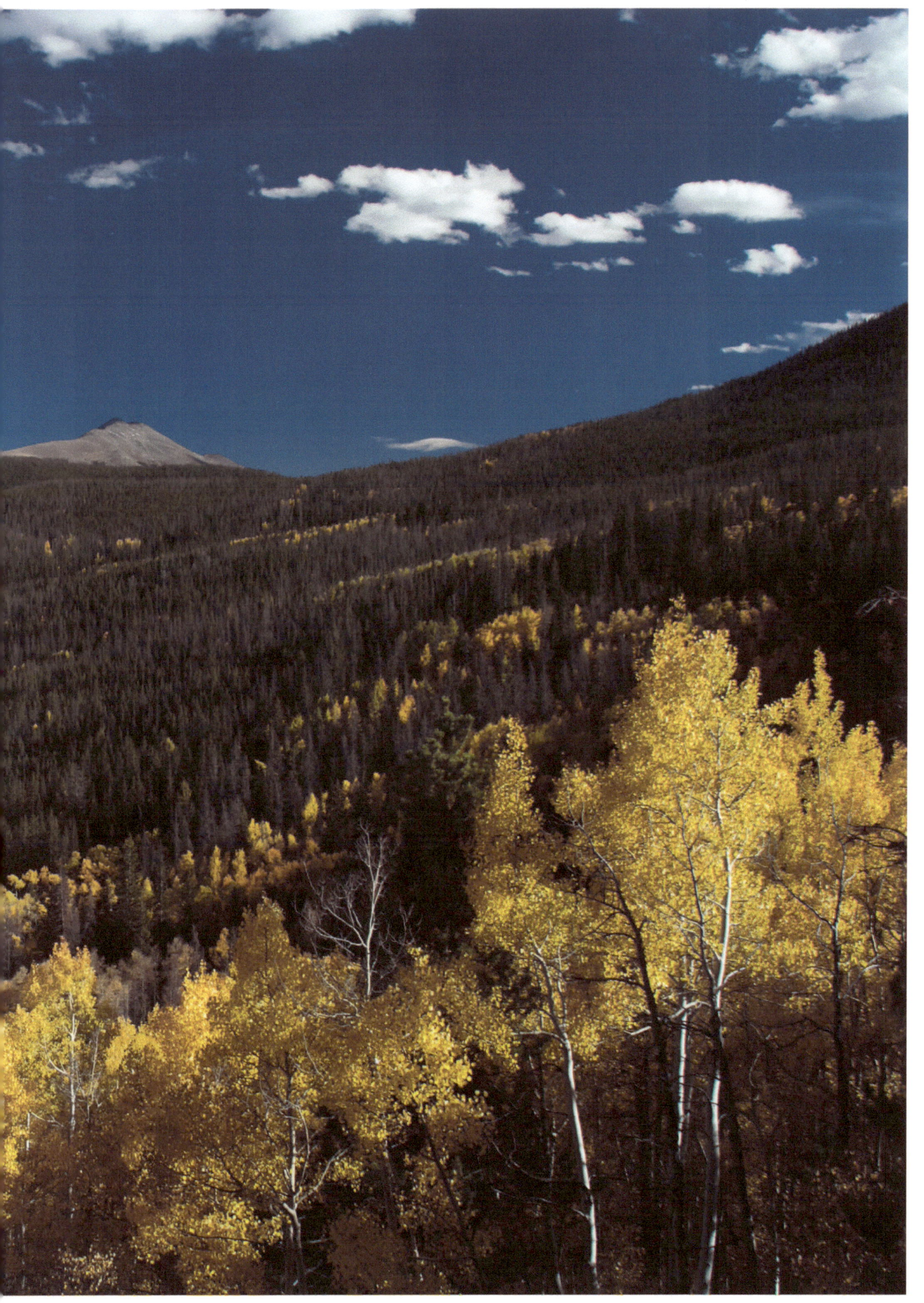

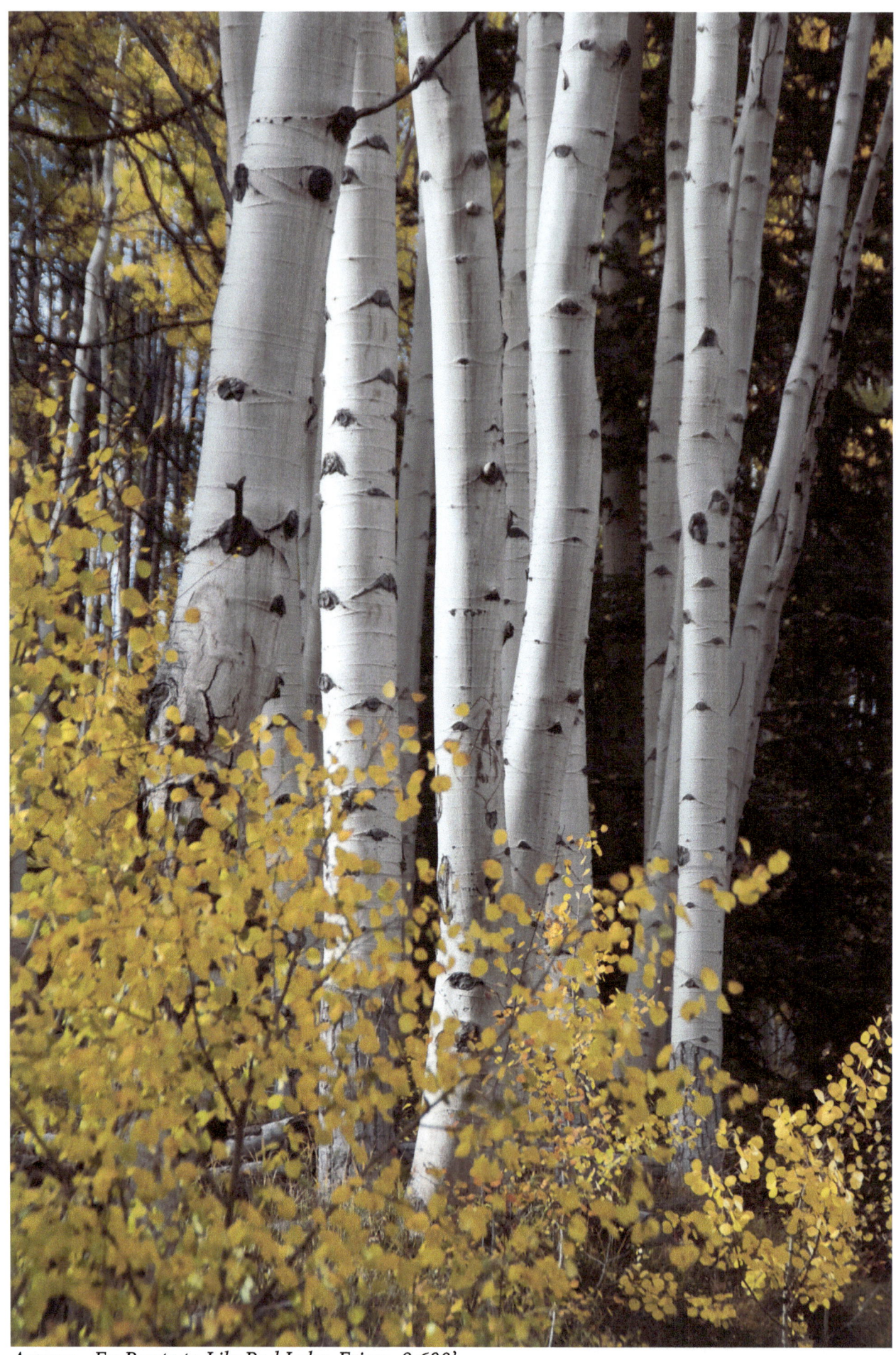

Aspens - En Route to Lily Pad Lake, Frisco, 9,600'

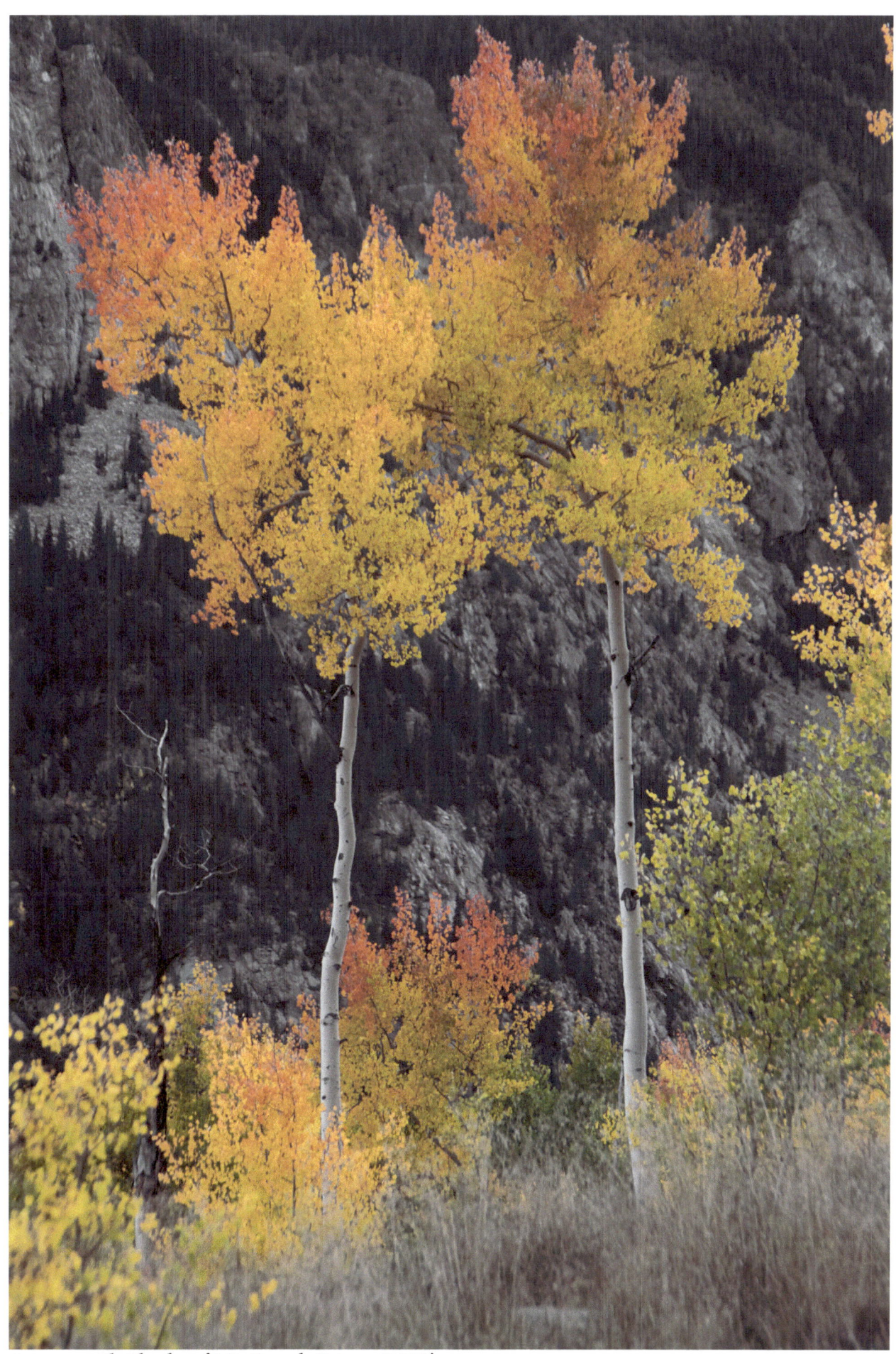

Aspens with Flanks of Mt. Royal, Frisco, 9,320'

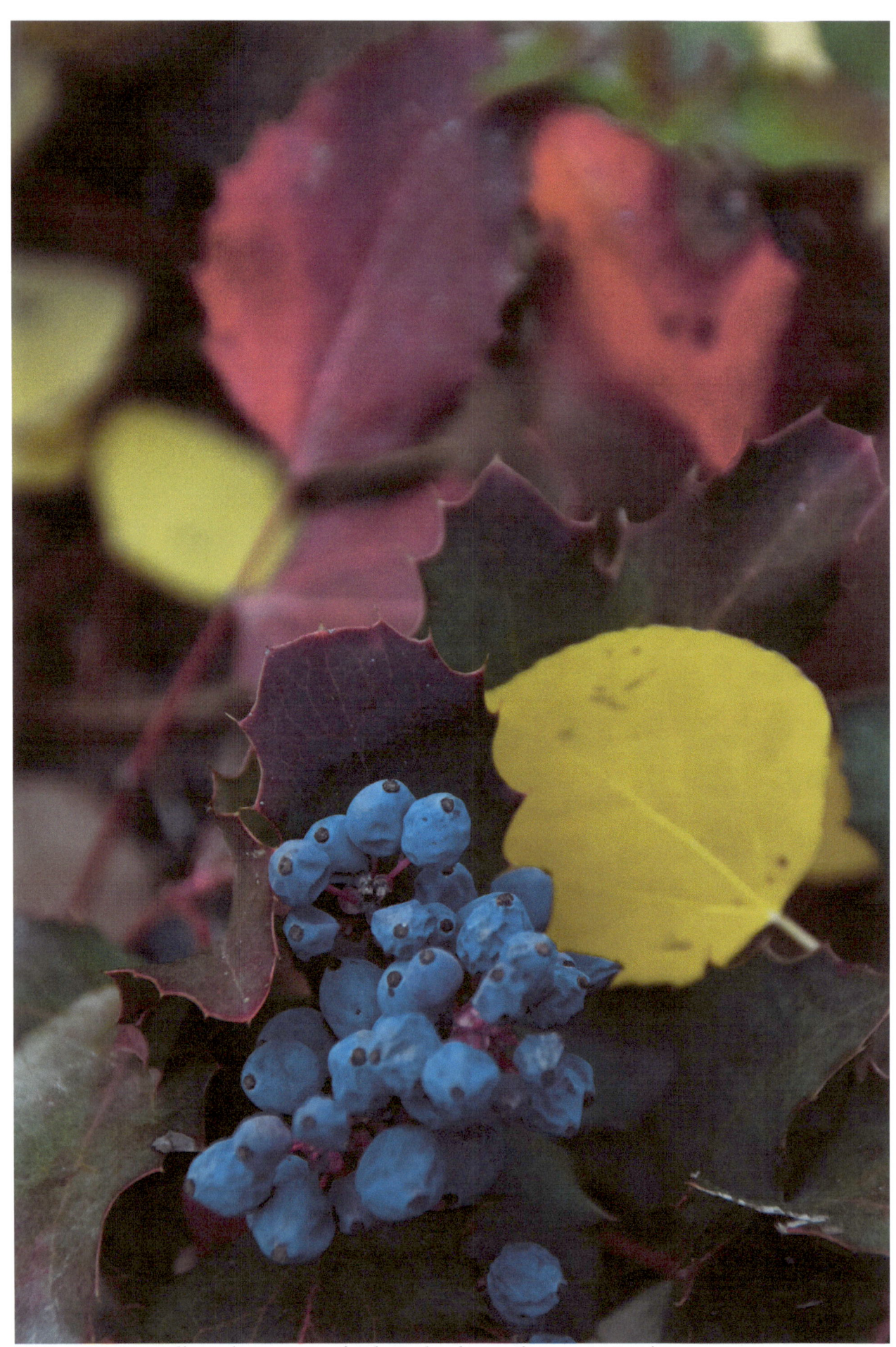

Oregon Grape Holly with Aspen Leaf, Lily Pad Lake Trail, Frisco, 9,880'

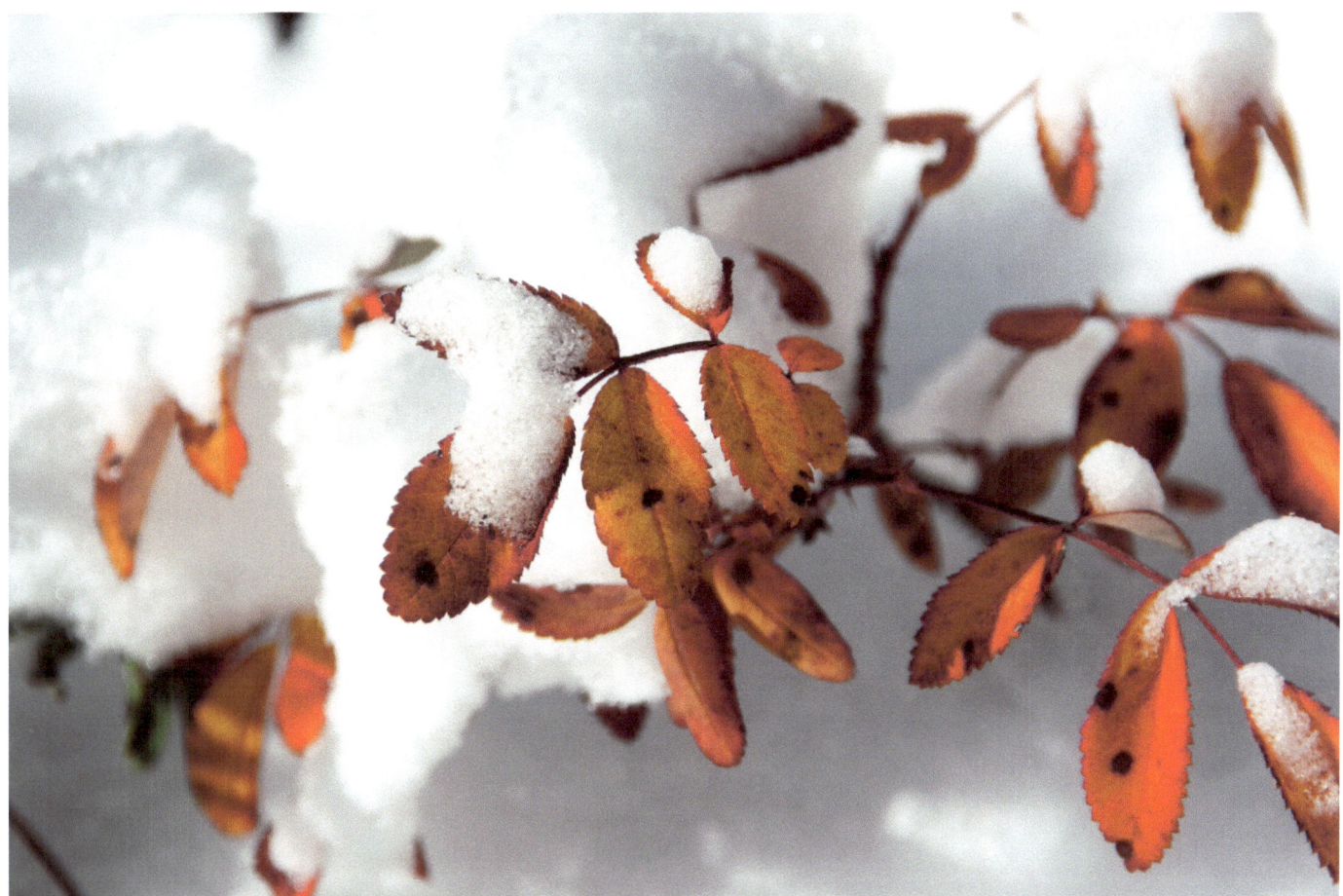

Wild Rose Bush with Snow, Frisco, 9,180'

As much as herbaceous underbrush sounds a subtle yet stern warning of impending autumn, perennial ground shrubs put on a show resisting and defying the inevitable. To the left, an Oregon Grape Holly is noted at almost 10,000 feet – displaying its fruit for the year – and reluctantly offering a tinge of color and some withering of its berries. This photo was taken October 4. Above a wild rose bush is finally letting go of the growth season – with a layer of fresh snow – taken October 6 slightly above 9000 feet. Note that the rose bush will not drop its leaves even under the weight of snow.

There is an irony to the defiance of these plants. Oregon Grape Hollies grow in rainy Oregon, in hot, moist, and shady sections of North Carolina – and yet I couldn't ever find one in New York – which was rainy and moist and a bit chilly. Colorado is a desert compared to all these places and far colder, yet they are wild.

The rose bush is another amusing example of meteorological stubbornness. I had a prolific and large rose garden in North Carolina. They demanded tons of water and sun – and shriveled at the site of shade. When the first frost came through, the leaves withered and fell. Again, here in Colorado, we find these rose bushes growing in shady areas, without extensive moisture, and defying cold temperatures. There is obviously a scientific explanation for the resilience of these plants – and I find value in their poetic defiance – science be damned. When I see these plants, I don't see a delicate antebellum damsel shining brilliantly in the sun, I see a leather-clad biker chick that is not to be messed with.

It is evident that these plants are very similar to people. Here we are the same species – and native North Carolinians thrive in the heat, sun, and torrential rains – while withering in any temperatures below 40 degrees. Local Coloradans find anyone who can't handle cold to be a drama queen, have some tolerance to summer heat, and wither at the thought of heat and humidity combined together.

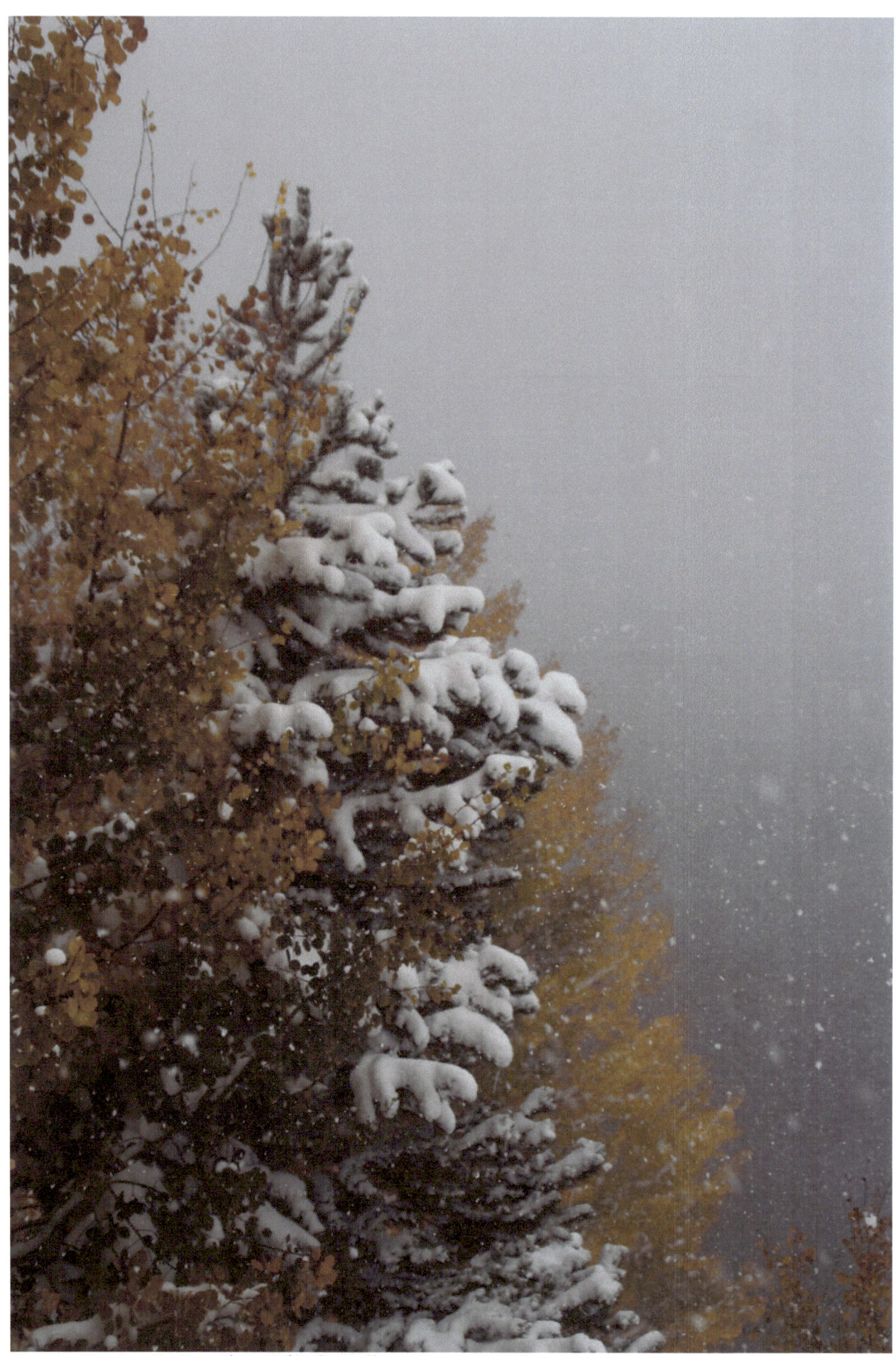

Aspens During Storm, Shore of Lake Dillon, Frisco, 9,020'

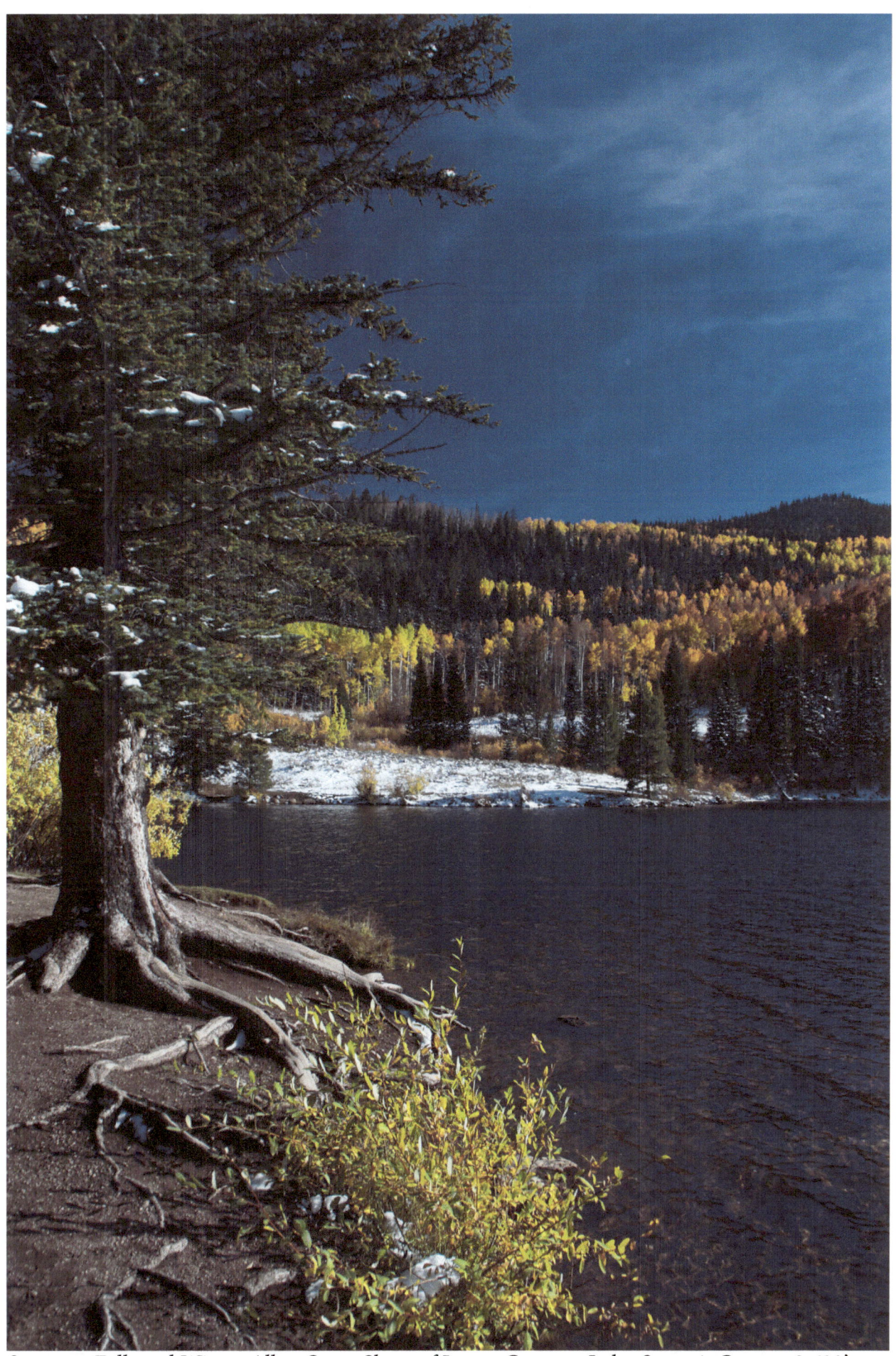

Summer, Fall, and Winter All at Once, Shore of Lower Cataract Lake, Summit County, 8,620'

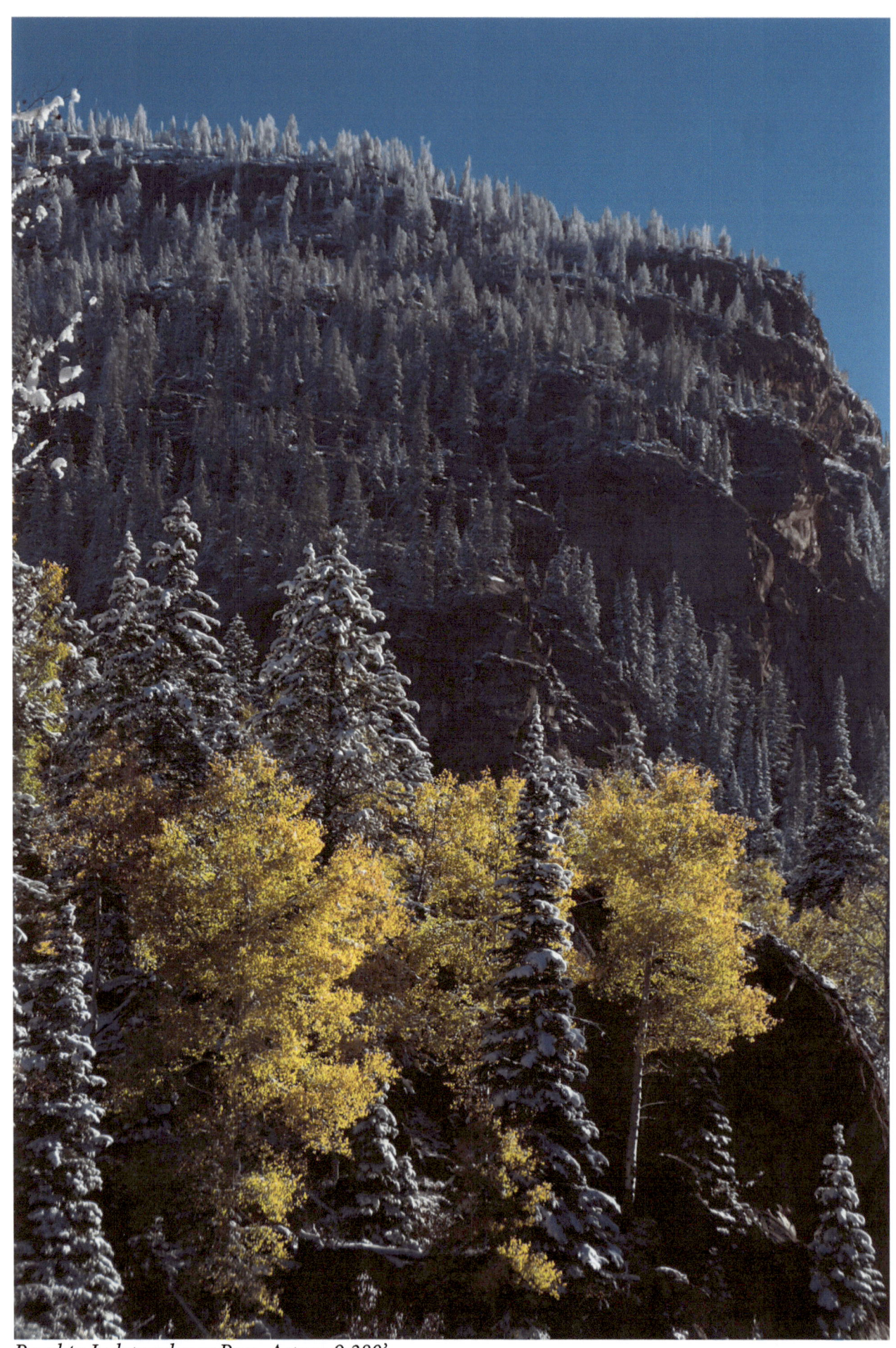

Road to Independence Pass, Aspen, 9,380'

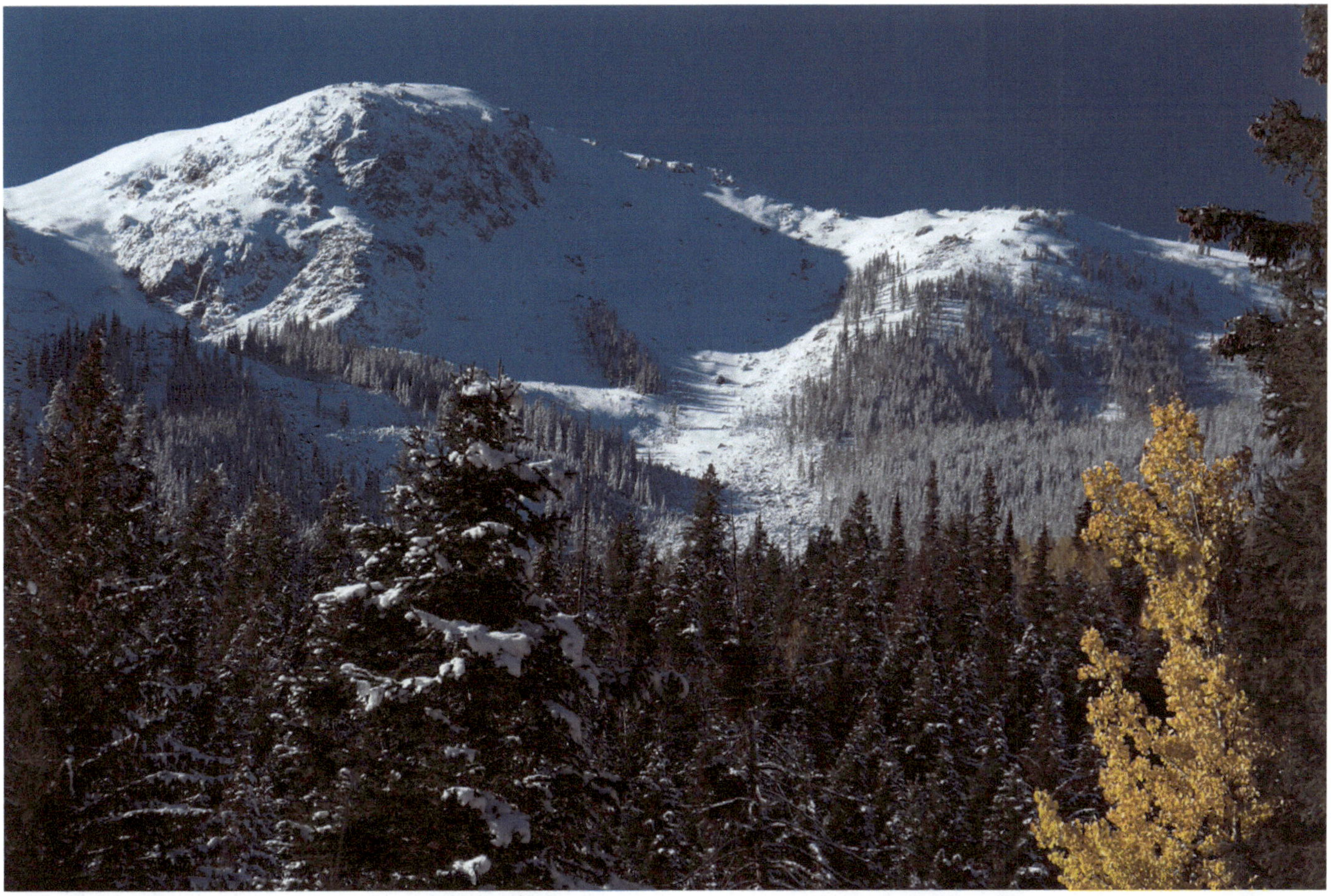

Road to Independence Pass, Aspen, 9,380'

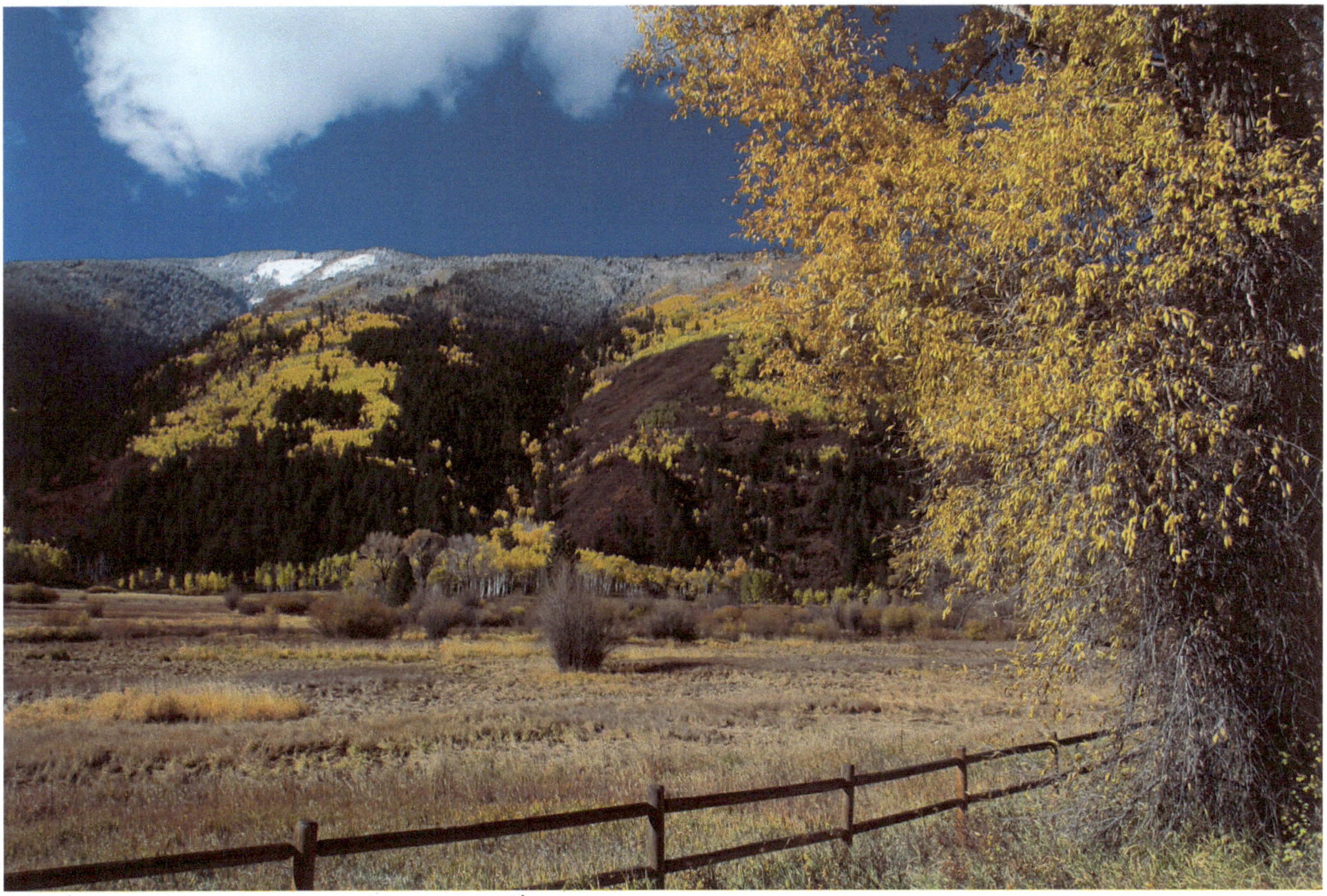

North Star Nature Preserve, Aspen, 8,020'

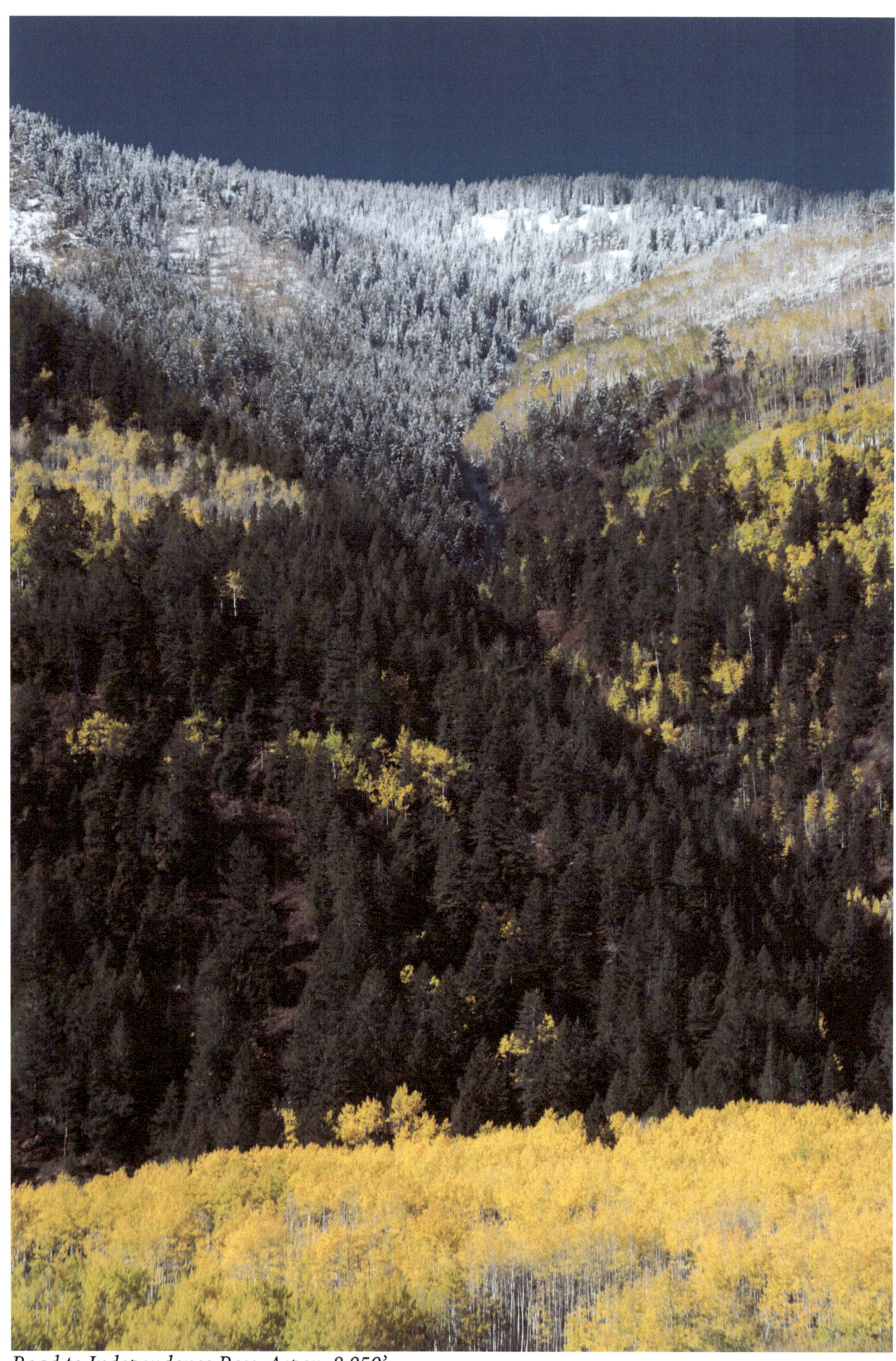

Road to Independence Pass, Aspen, 8,050'

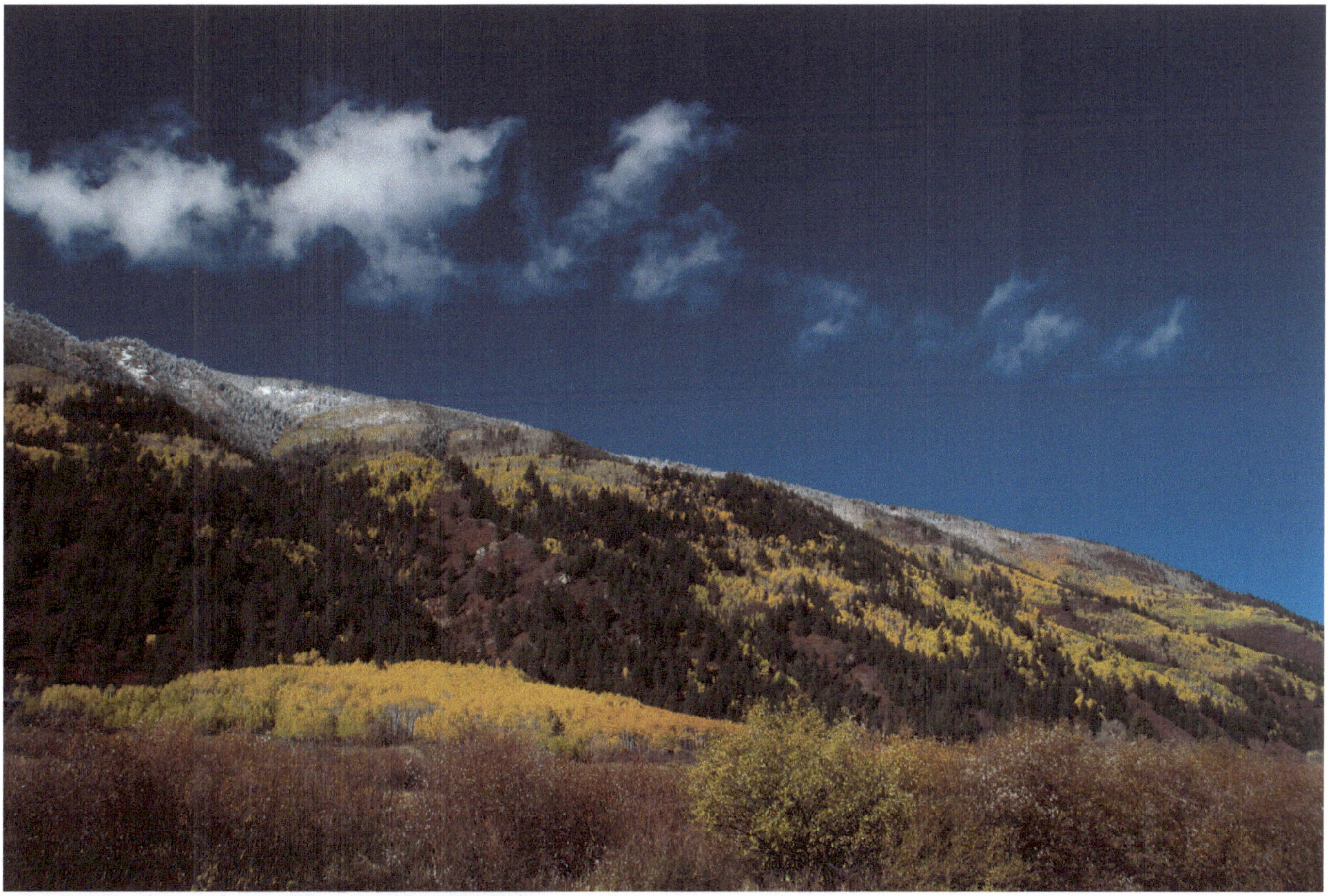

Road to Independence Pass, Aspen, 8,060'

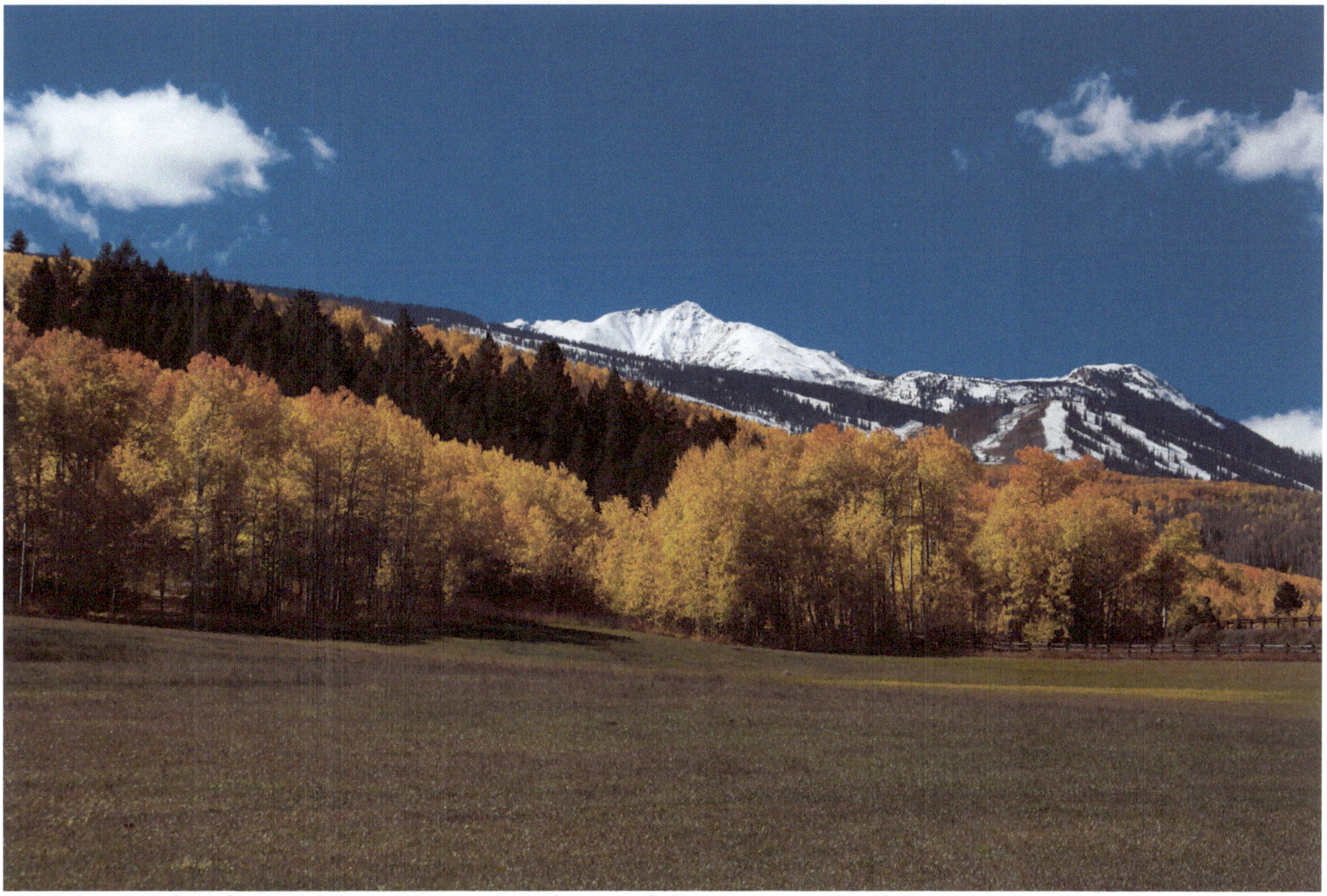

Owl Creek Rd with Snowmass Resort in Background, Snowmass, 8,320'

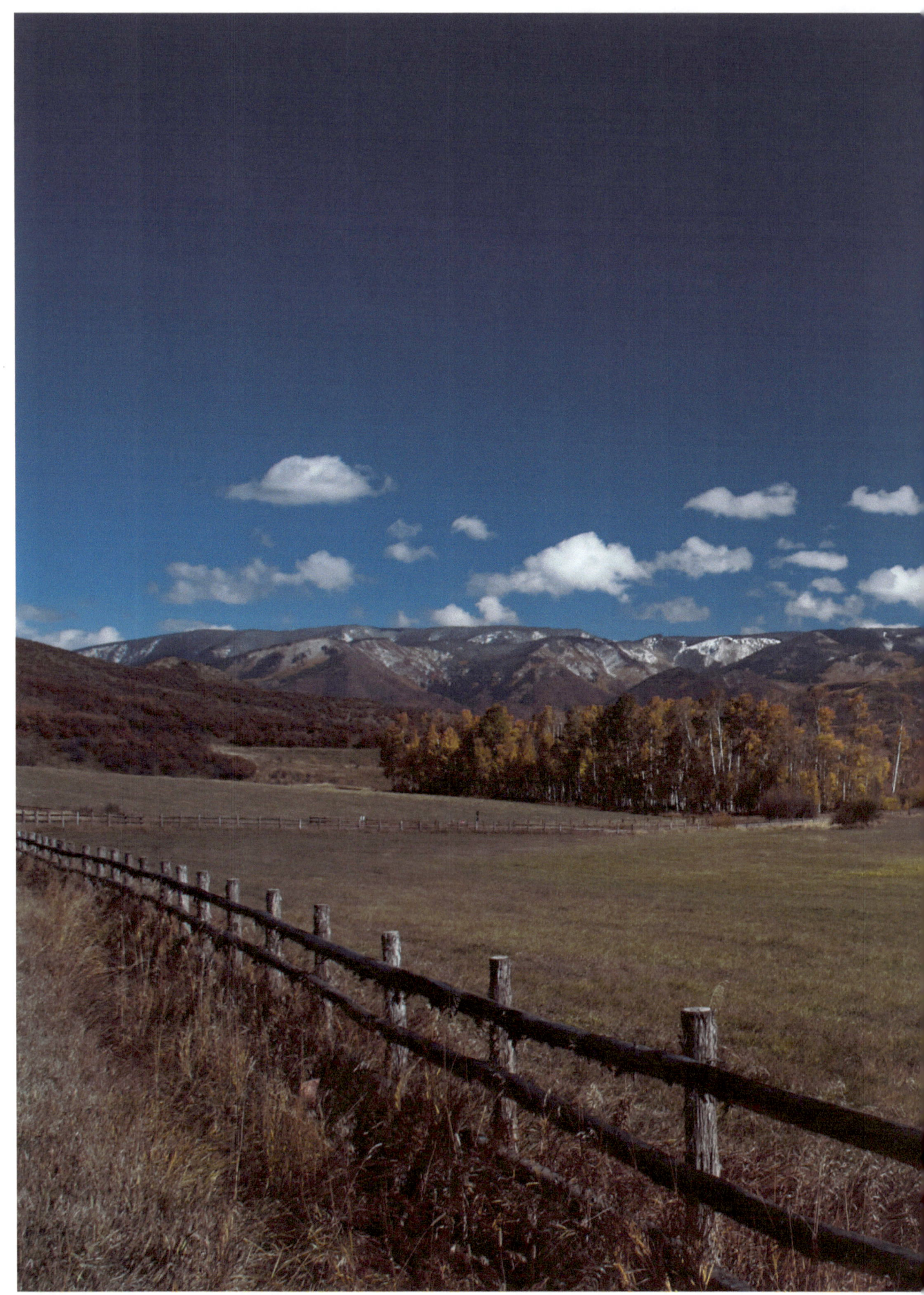

Owl Creek Rd, Snowmass, 8,350'

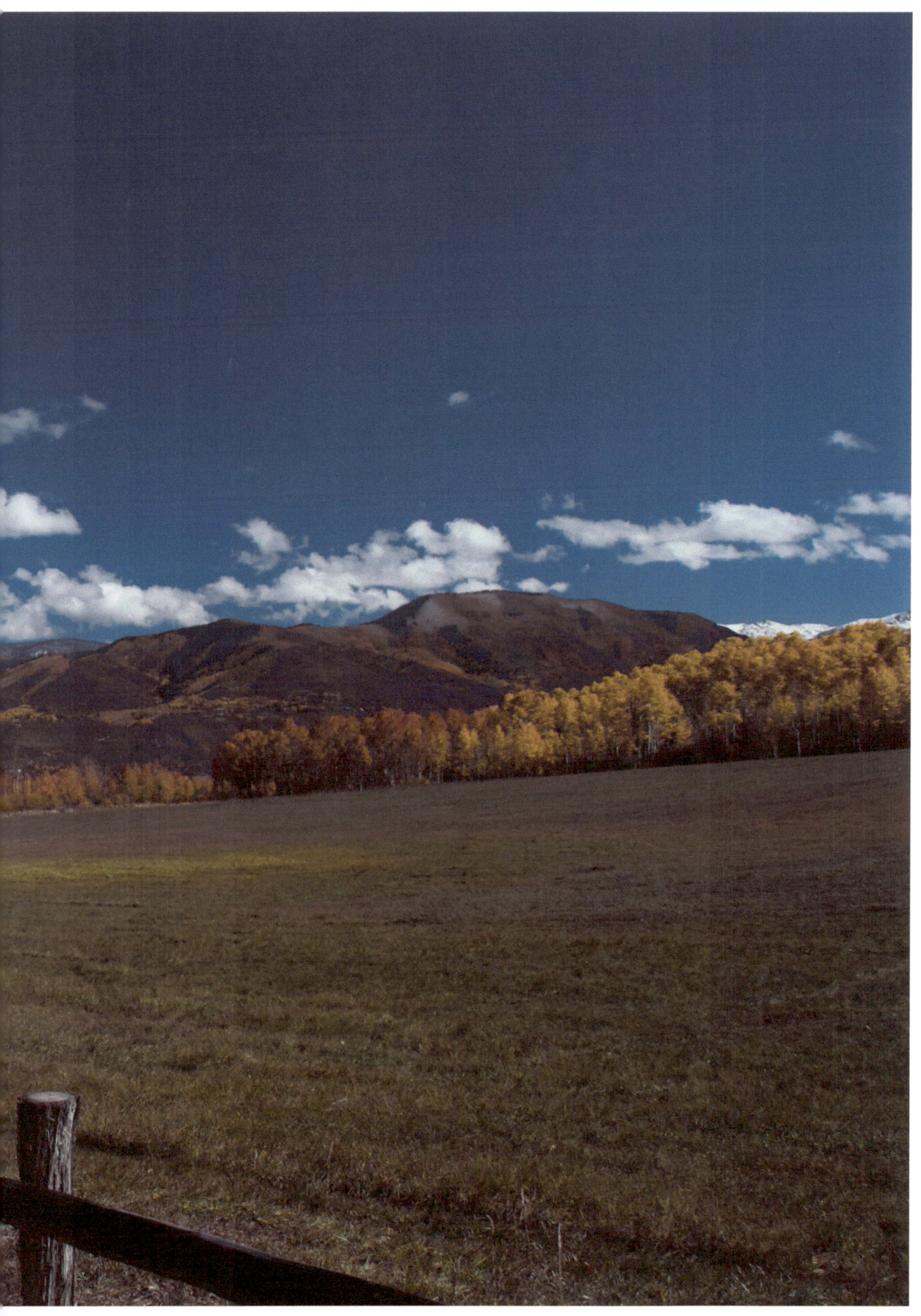

I am a purist when it comes to my photos. I consider most human influence to be a murky cesspool of developed infection; hence, I specifically shriek and avoid it when trying to photo beauty. In this particular case, Aspen lay before me in resplendent beauty with a dark blue sky, epic foreground, and beautiful village. What do to about that steel machination known as a "ski lift?" Well, in a rare testament to the human experience, I decided to keep it. Aspen is the quintessential experience of opulent comfort while bathing in the rawness of Western wilderness. Skiing in Aspen gave us that archetype – so in a moment of rareness, a human construction has been included.

Even more amusing was how I came to discover this location. The previous day, I had asked some locals if there was anywhere up Castle Creek Rd where I could see some aspens before the sun went down. Someone suggested driving up Midnight Mine Rd. "You should see some aspens from there. It will take you to the top of Aspen Mountain, but I doubt you'll get there due to the snow and steepness." When it comes to heights, I am like a cat. If I can go higher, I will. So I did. Up I went from 7,900 feet, curving up the mountain, and eventually ran into a little snow at 10,000 feet. "A little" become "some more" at 10,500 and I then had some incredible views of the massive peaks south of Aspen. Further, it looked like I had climbed the stairway to heaven. "Well, it looks like the top is over that way. Let me see what is there." Ruts turned into snow-covered road – and I reached the top of the ridge at roughly 11,200

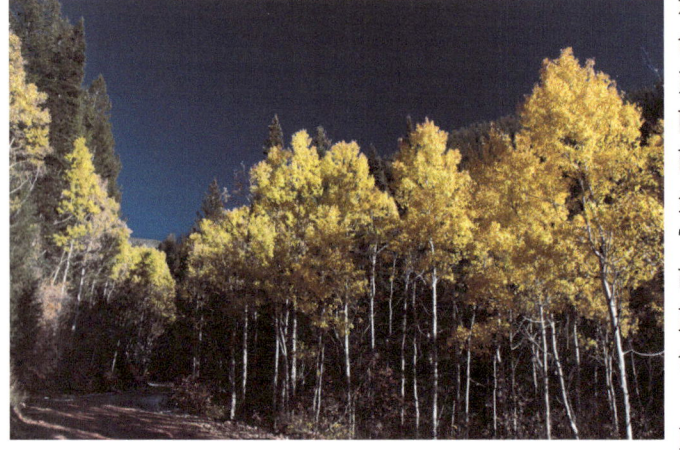

Midnight Mine Rd, Aspen, 8,770'

feet – revealing a view of epic magnitude. I sensed that the top of Aspen Mountain couldn't be too far north – so I traversed along for some time in 4x4 to make it possible. I had a lingering thought of "what if I have to drive back down that slushy insanity?" "Well, it will hopefully freeze the ruts in place which is better than wet slush." The tracks of previous off-road drivers lessened, followed by merely ATV tracks, followed by no tracks. The road location was relatively obvious – and with only about 4" to 6" of snow on the road, it didn't seem so bad.

I came to a descent. As I crept down and went around a curve, it became evident that, much like a cat that has climbed a tall tree, this was a stupid idea. In 4x4, I put it in reverse. All 4 wheels spun. To my left was a drop off – to the right an embankment. In front of me was a rather steep descent – to where I am was not sure – and there was a snow-covered washout in between me and the unknown. Giving it some thought, I realized AAA would not tow me up there – and that my options were to wait 2 days (up there, camping) for it to melt or to proceed forward. Ever so slowly I crept forward – and gave it a little gas to zoom past the washout. The risk was sliding sideways off the ledge to the side as the road was iced over. Fortunately I did not. Instead, I slid down the road – into the loving arms of a flat area with additional tracks that had come from "somewhere else."

That "somewhere else" was in the direction of Aspen Mountain. "What comes up must go down, so this should work." Indeed it did – as within 5 minutes, the top of the Silver Queen gondola was gracing my windshield. I was aware that the descent would be interesting – as I have seen Aspen Mountain from the village – and it is steep – steep enough that skiing parts of it gives me pause.

Proceeding forward, the initial section of the hill is benign. However, the "road" (read: harsh 4x4 trail) is snow-covered and icy and I have summer tires. Not all season radials – summer tires purchased for high-speed highway driving in metropolitan North Carolina – hardly for above timberline, steep, winter off-roading. Nonetheless, I could leave the truck for the winter – or drive down.

There were sections where the road was so steep, I would ride the ABS brakes down and essentially do a controlled slide to the next shallow angle area. After getting used to this little exercise (believe it or not one actually can become accustomed to such a thing) – especially alongside precipices representing double diamond runs, the snow line was reached at about 10,500 feet – and the road became more hospitable….. for about a half mile. Then the steep section hit with a fury. There were sections where I had it in first gear, 4x4 low, and was riding the brakes at 3,000 rpm. For those that do not know, 4x4 low engages gearing in the transfer case that makes the engine turn at extremely fast RPMs even at a snail's pace. It is used in extreme situations when high torque is needed to climb steep inclines or to descend cliffs.

At times, my seatbelt was locked merely from the angle of the road – and I was effectively hanging from it – as I needed the support to keep the endurance to remain upright to drive. Again, this little routine became normal. Steep got steeper – and it seemed to not be a big deal. After getting to the bottom, I went from off-road 4x4 muddy-truck redneckism and entered into what is probably a $3 million to $5 million neighborhood of slope-side condos – followed by the village itself.

At this point, it was dark, so I decided to go back up the next morning when the sun was right. As I was ascending in 4x4 low, I realized what I had gotten myself into – as I was having a serious concern about engine overheat and sufficient traction to make it up. The stress on a vehicle to climb such a rough road, with so many hairpins, at such a steep angle, for such a distance was unlike anything I had ascended before. All for the photo (as usual)! And then I went back down it again.

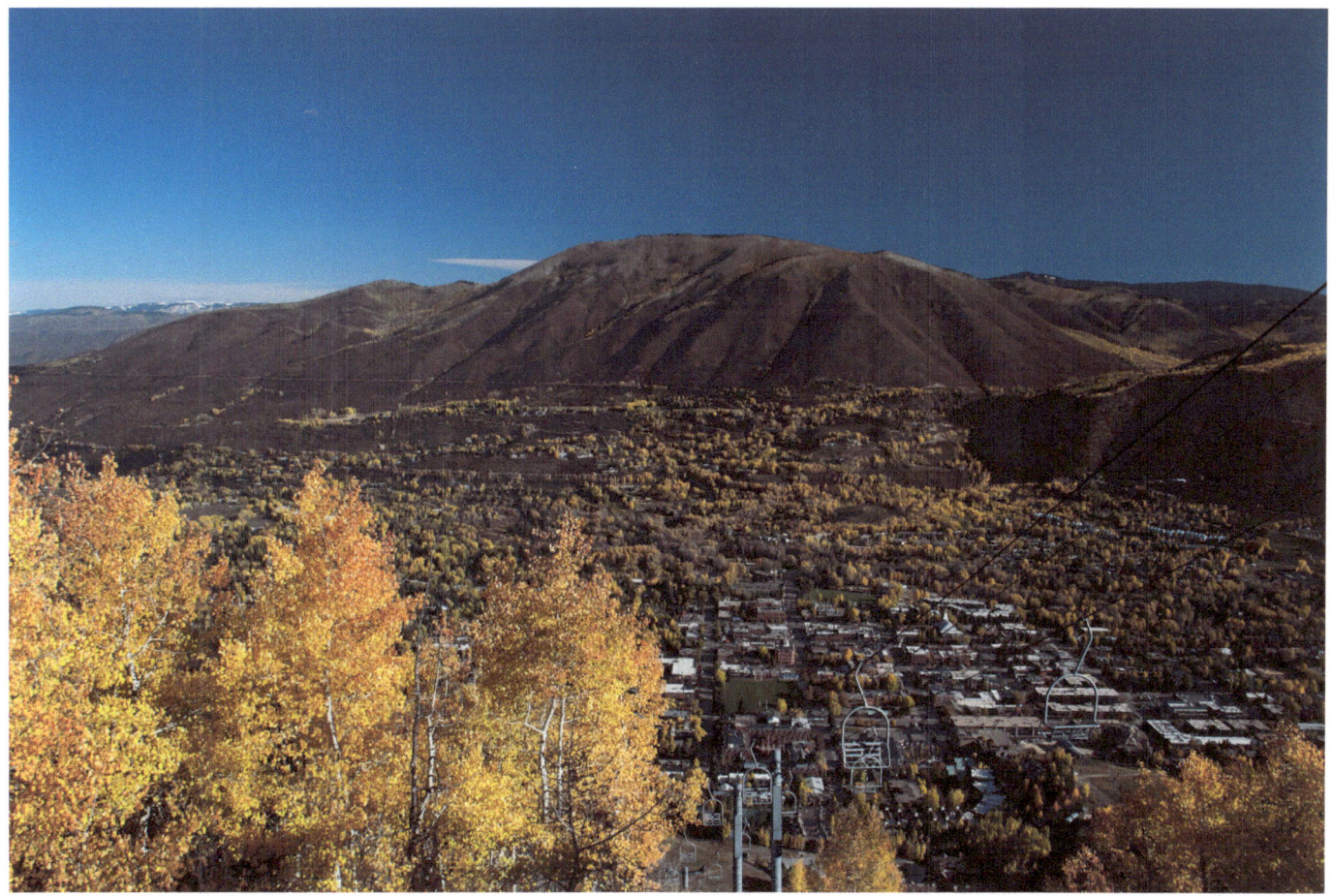

Aspen Village from Aspen Mountain, 9,040'

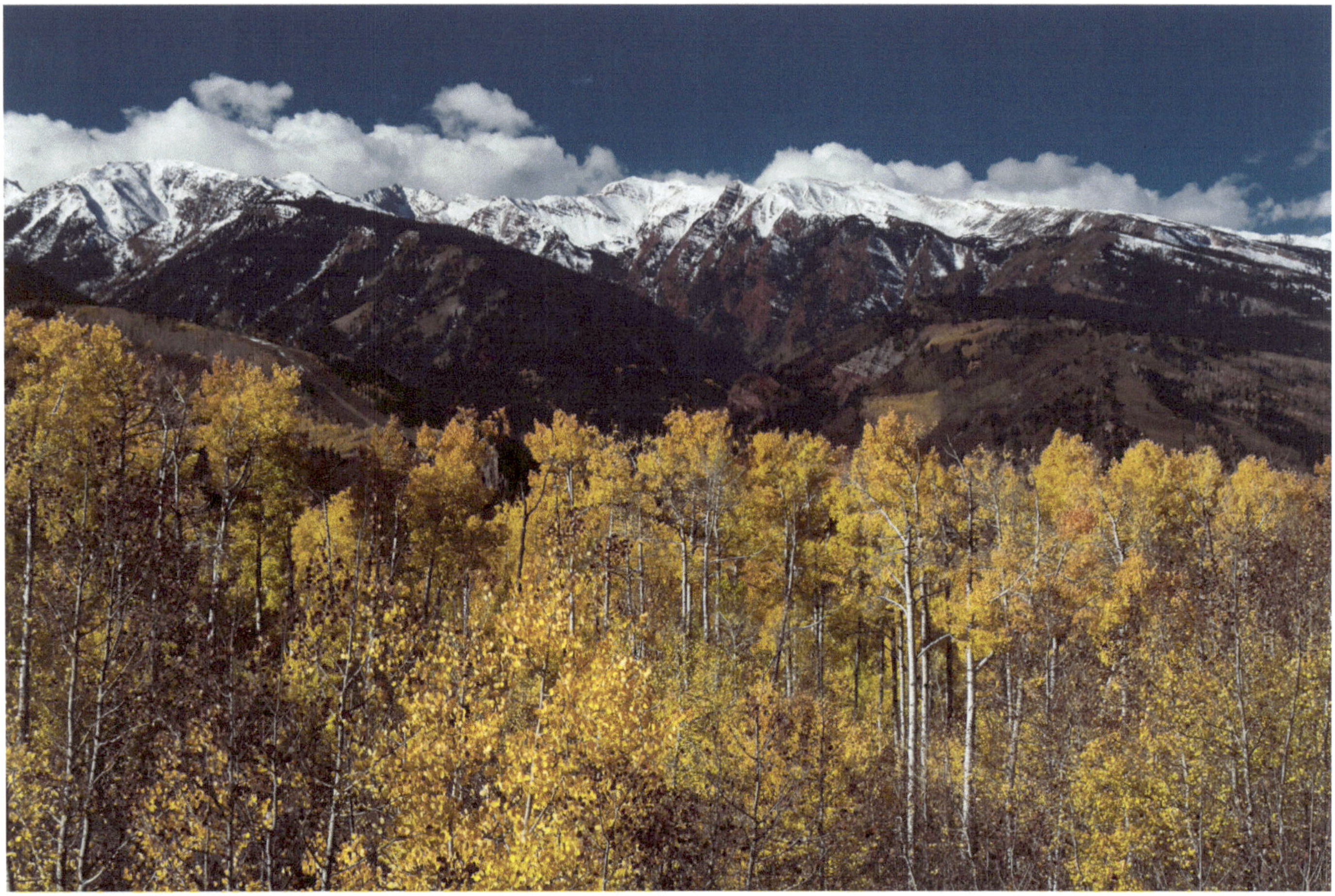

View from Smuggler Mtn Rd, Aspen, 9,020'

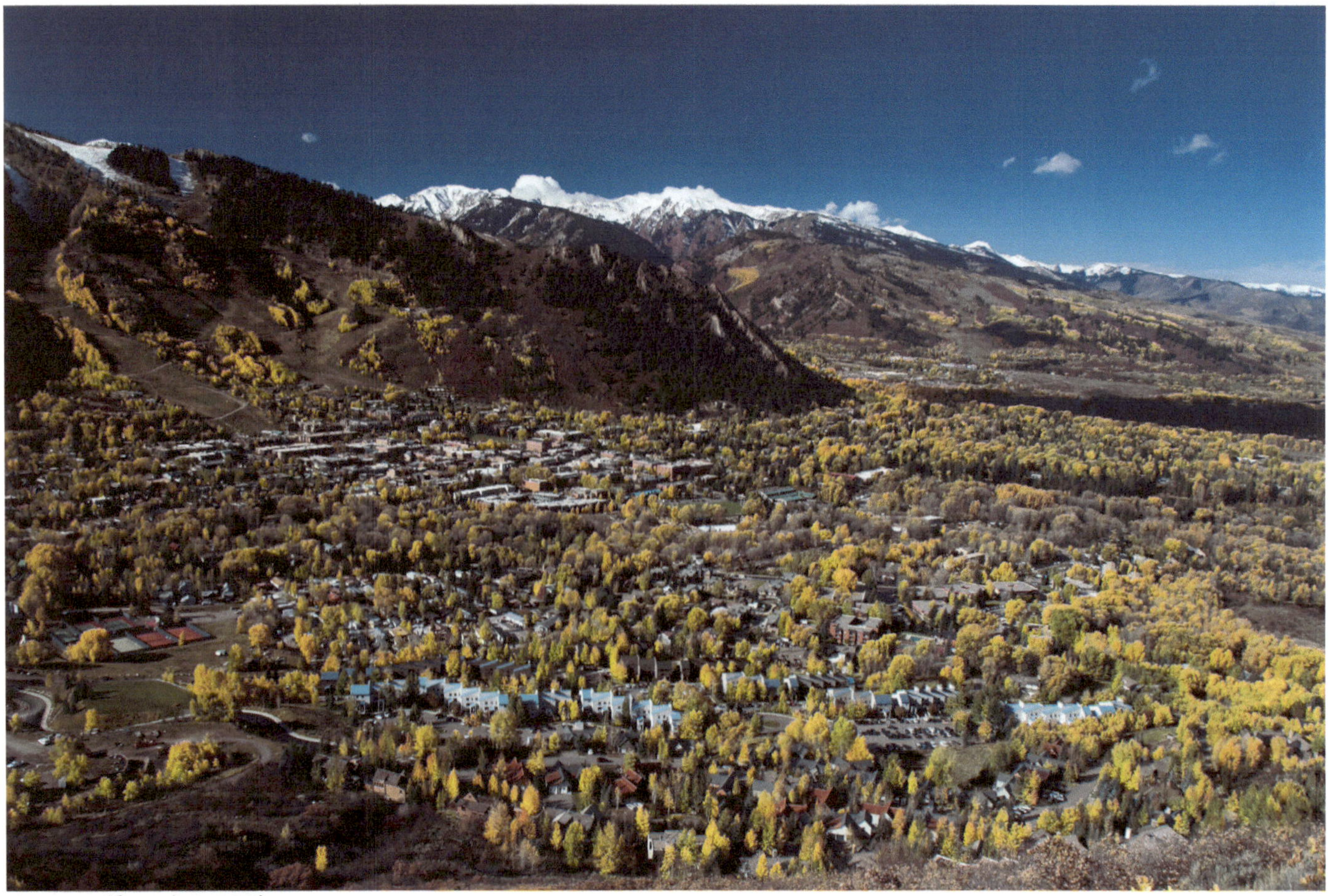

Aspen, (from) 8,580'

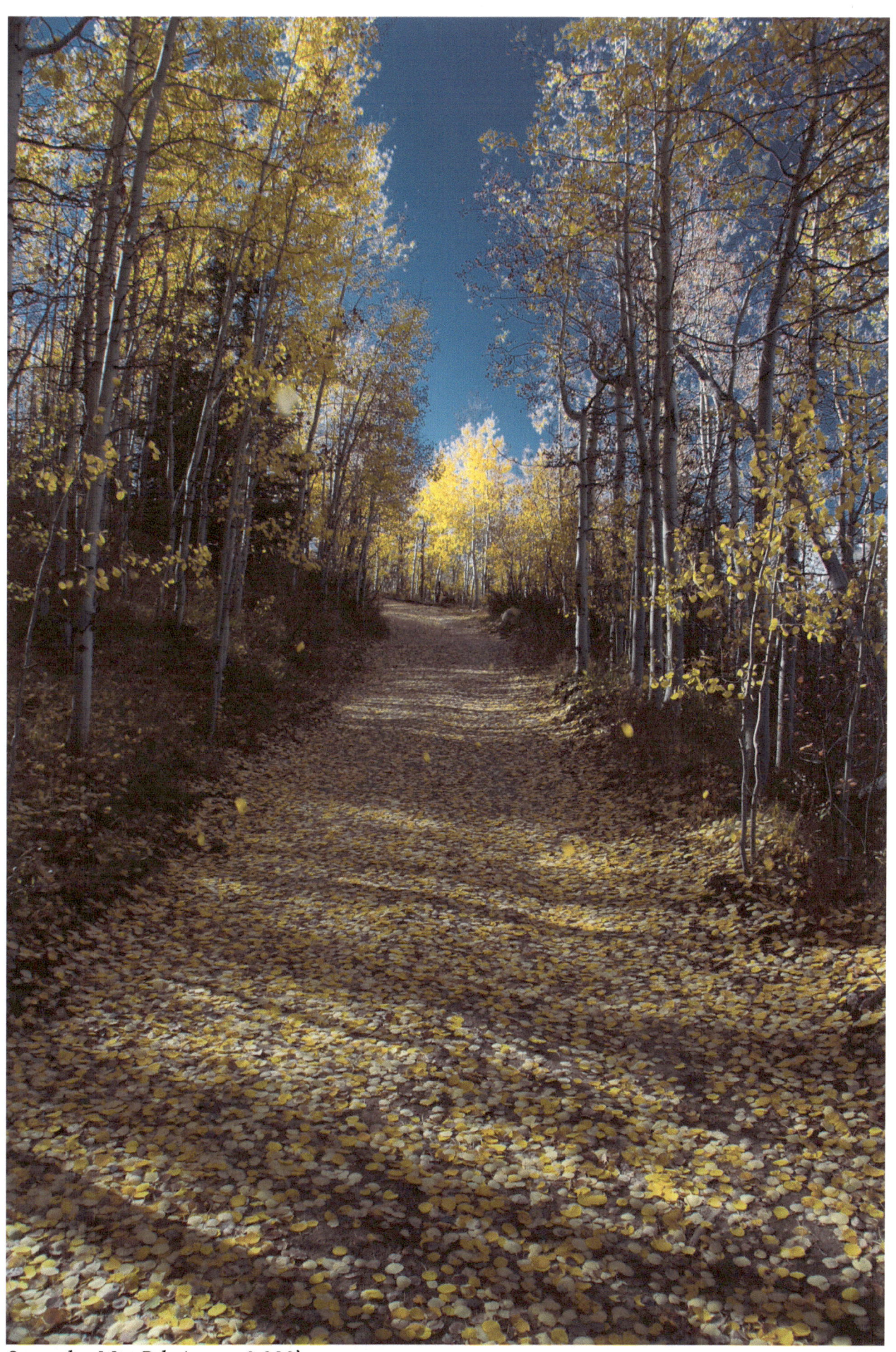

Smuggler Mtn Rd, Aspen, 8,880'

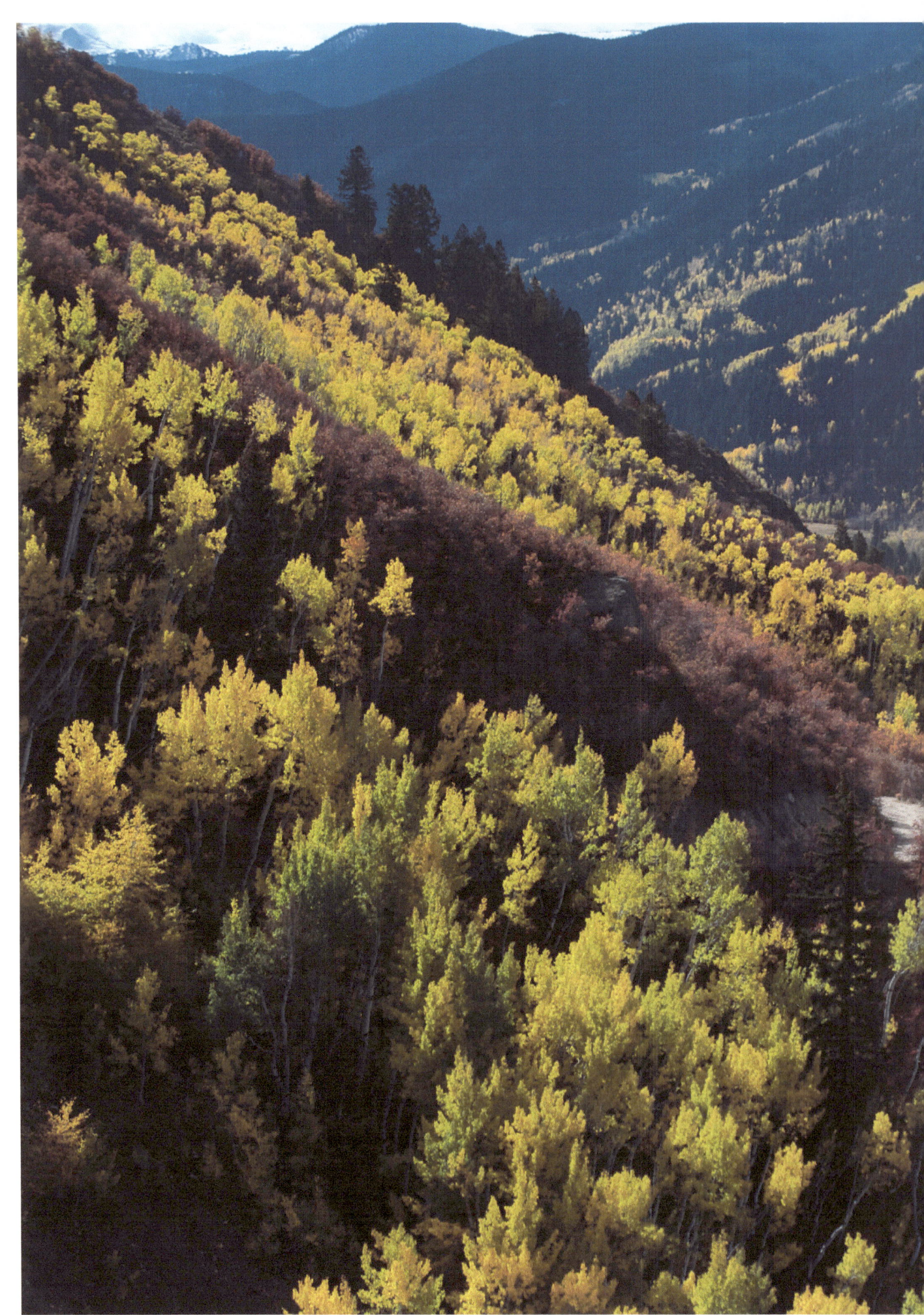

Upper Roaring Fork Valley, East of Aspen, 8,600'

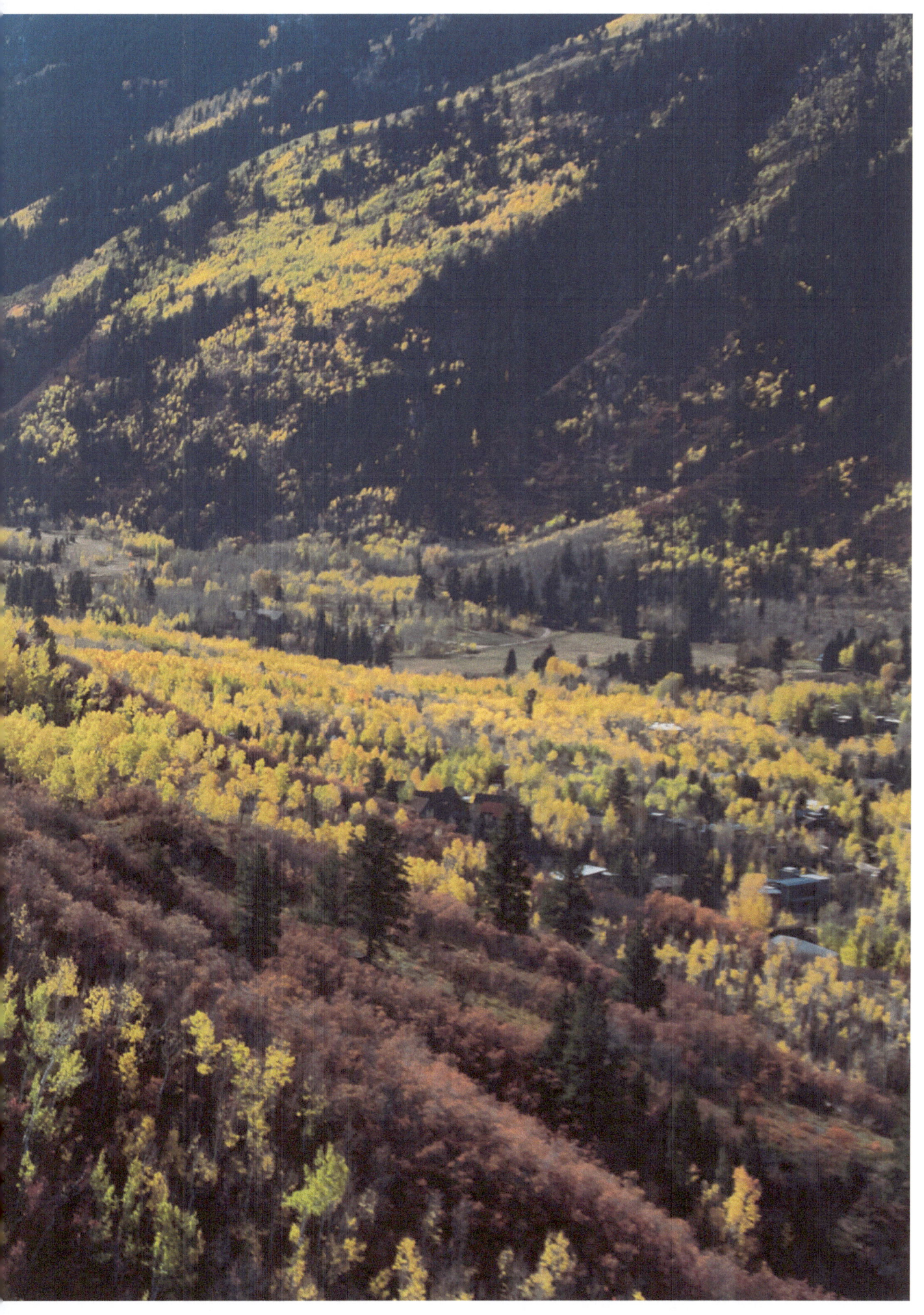

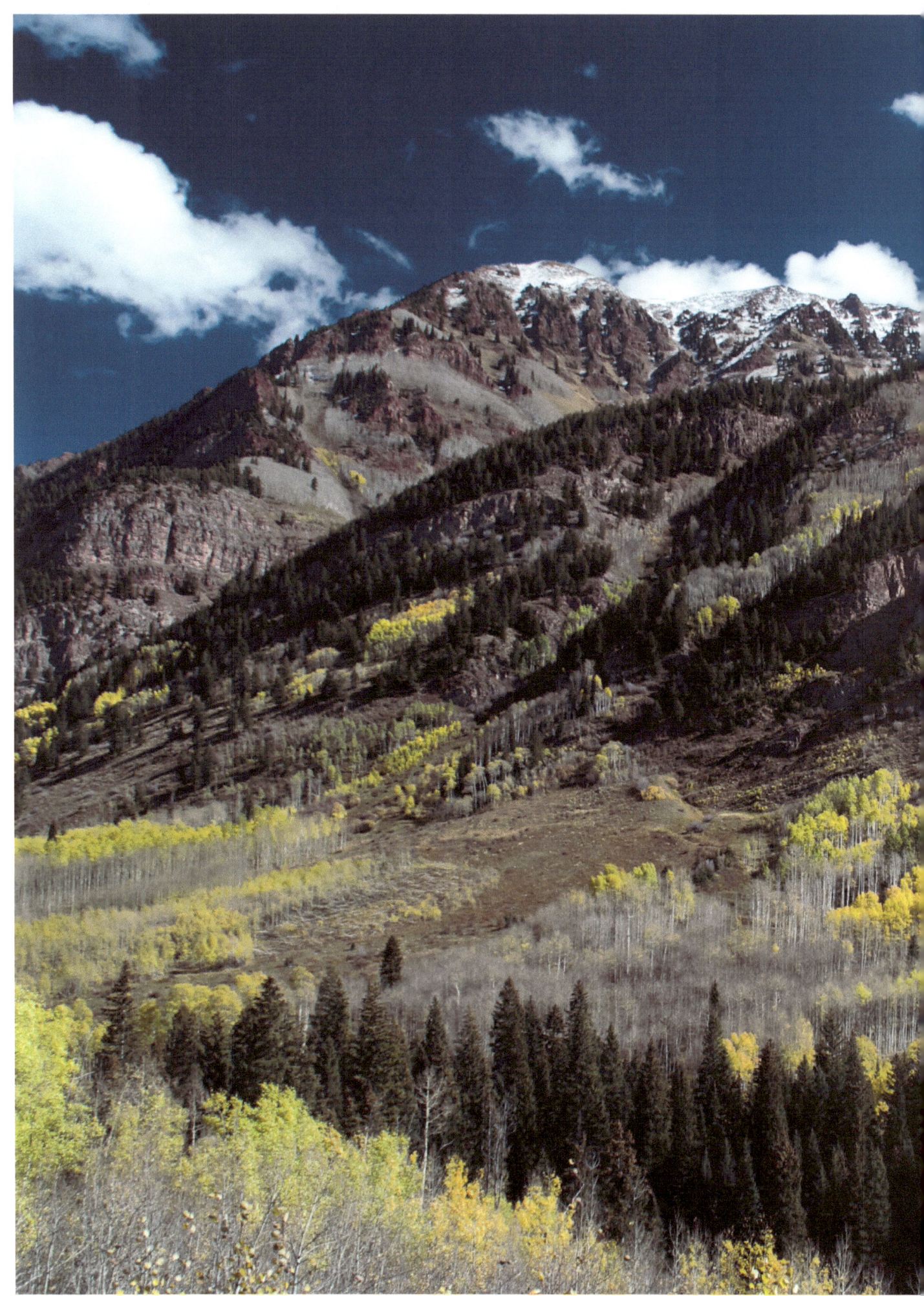

Maroon Creek Rd, Aspen, 8,820'

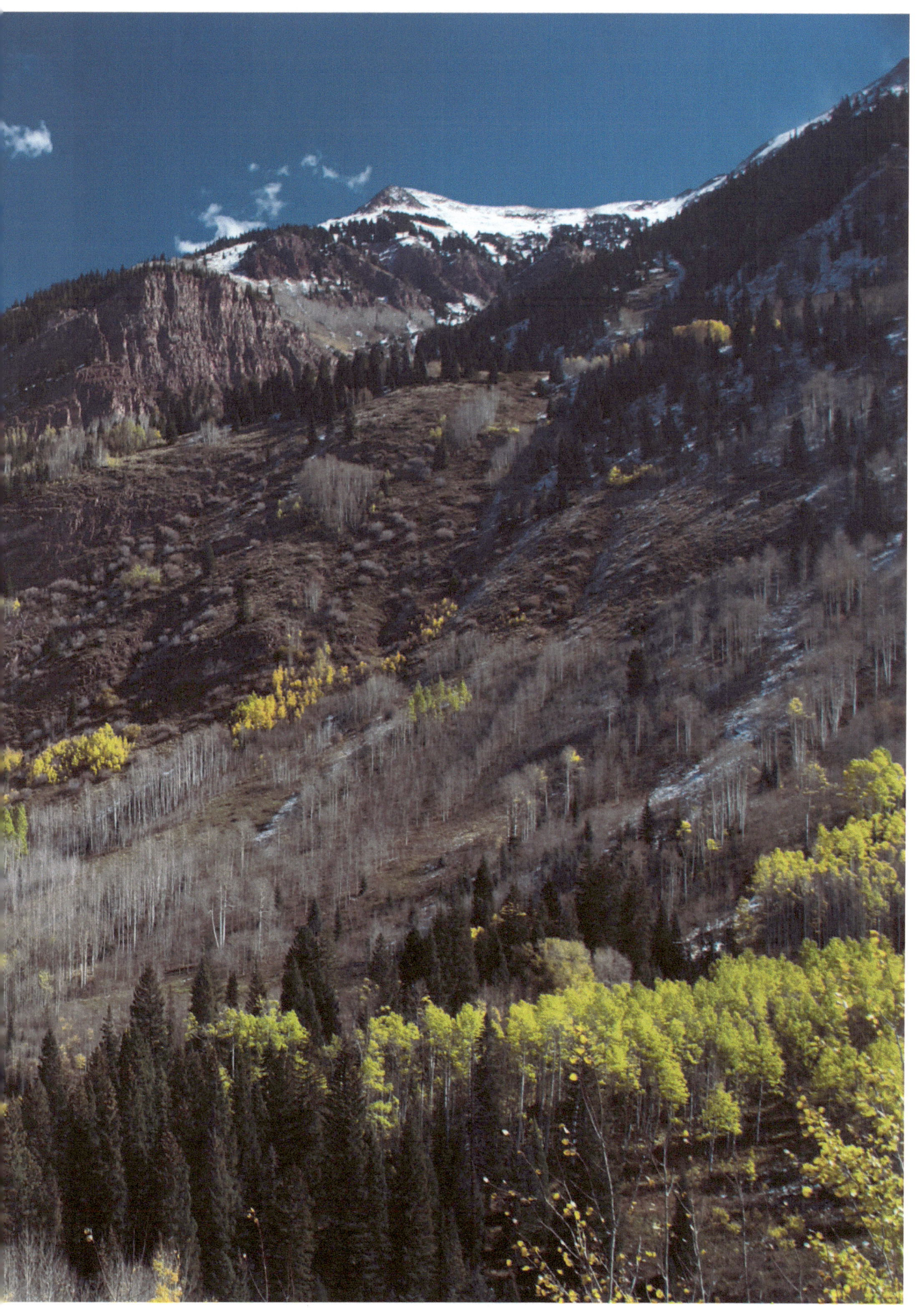

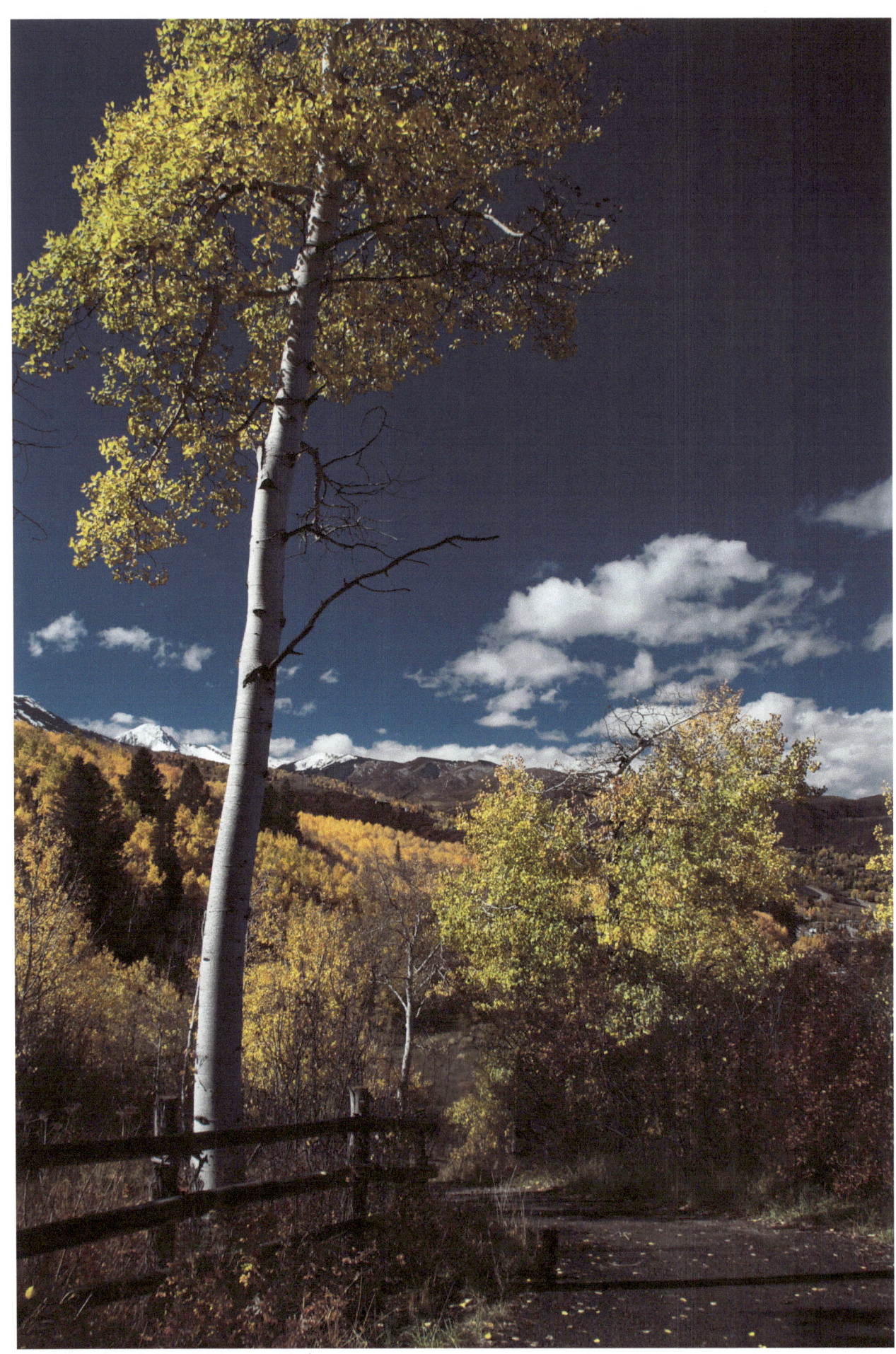

Owl Creek Rd, Snowmass, 8,360'

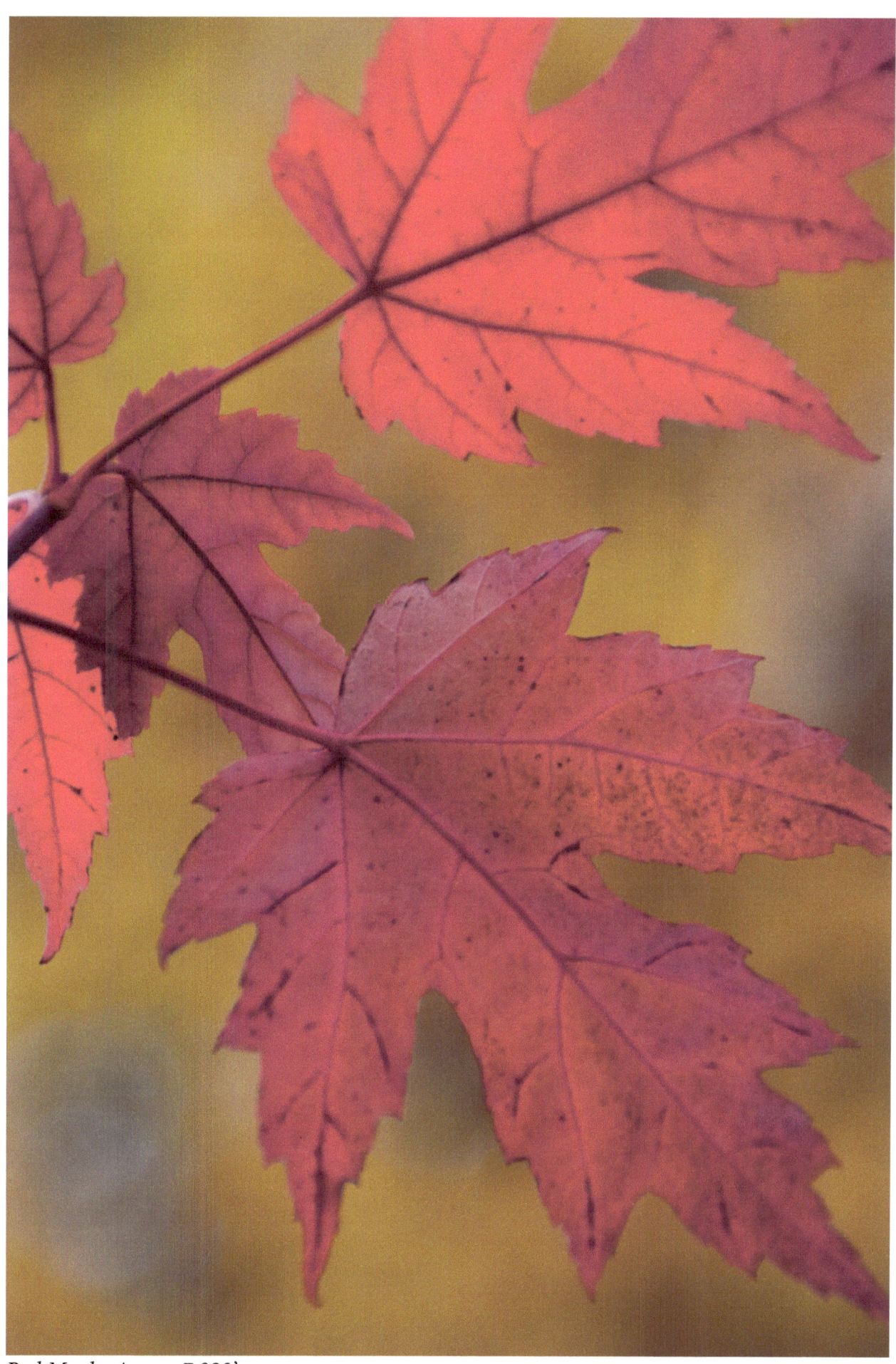

Red Maple, Aspen, 7,890'

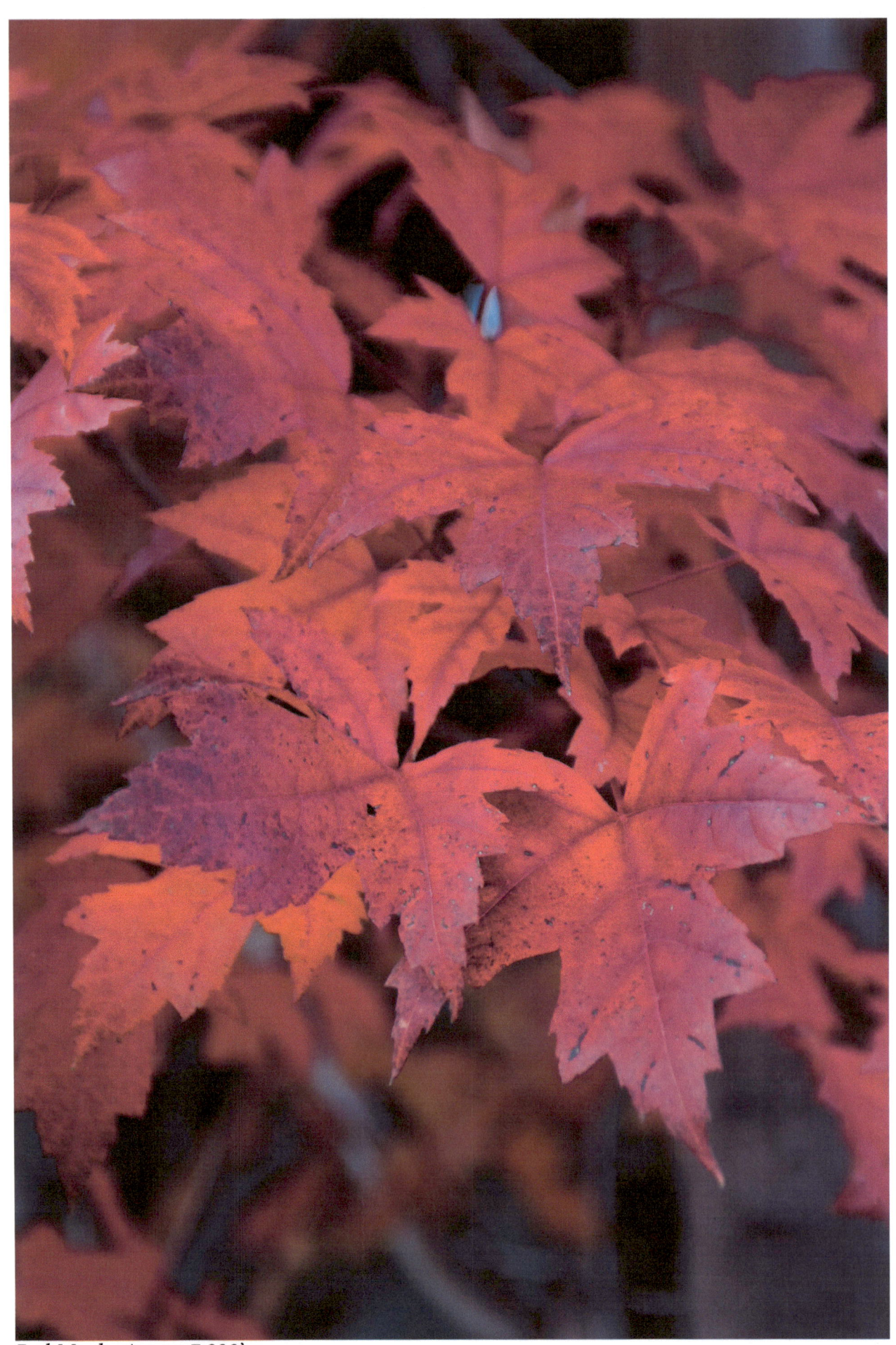

Red Maple, Aspen, 7,890'

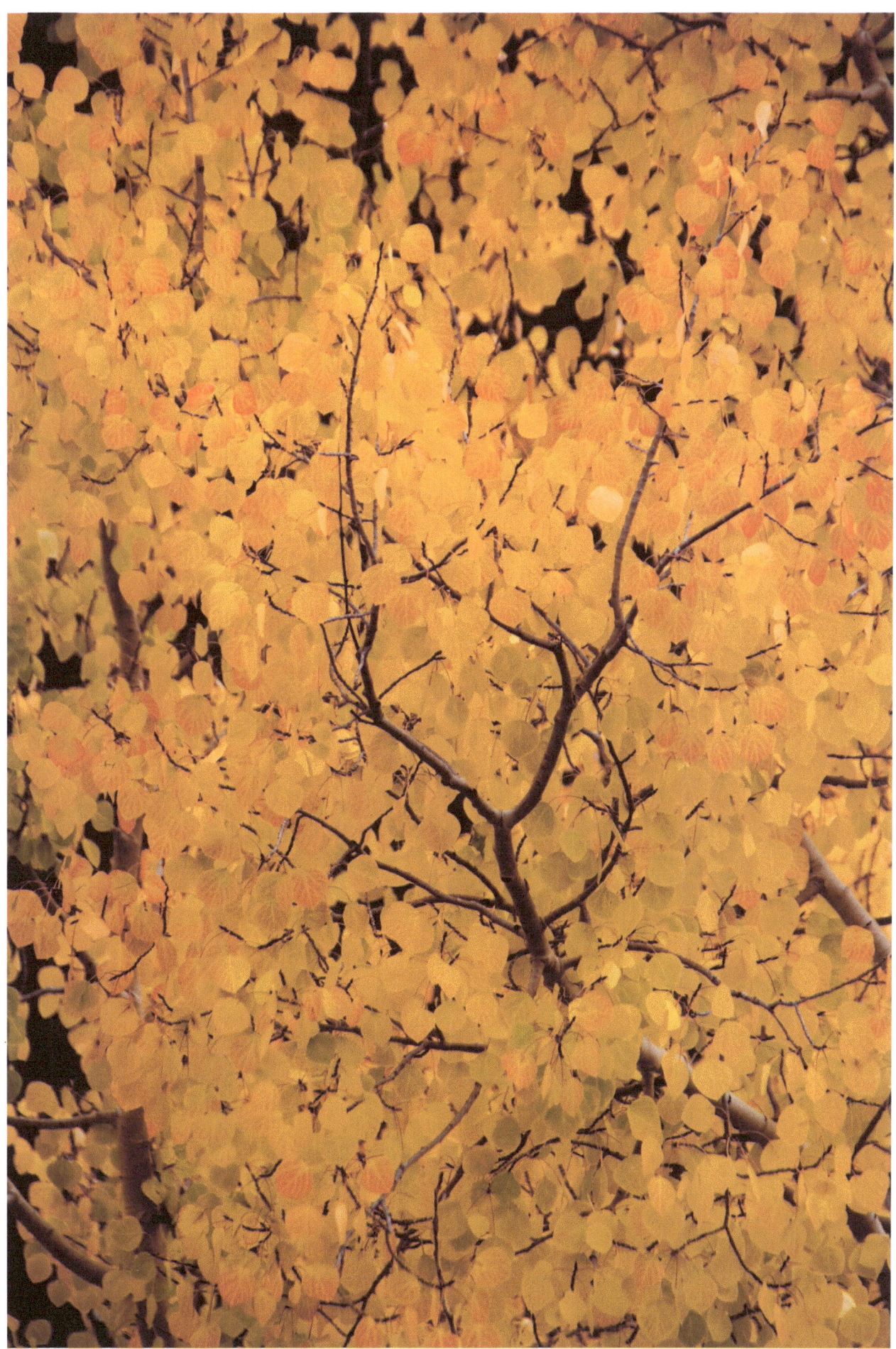

Boreas Pass Rd, Breckenridge, 10,410'

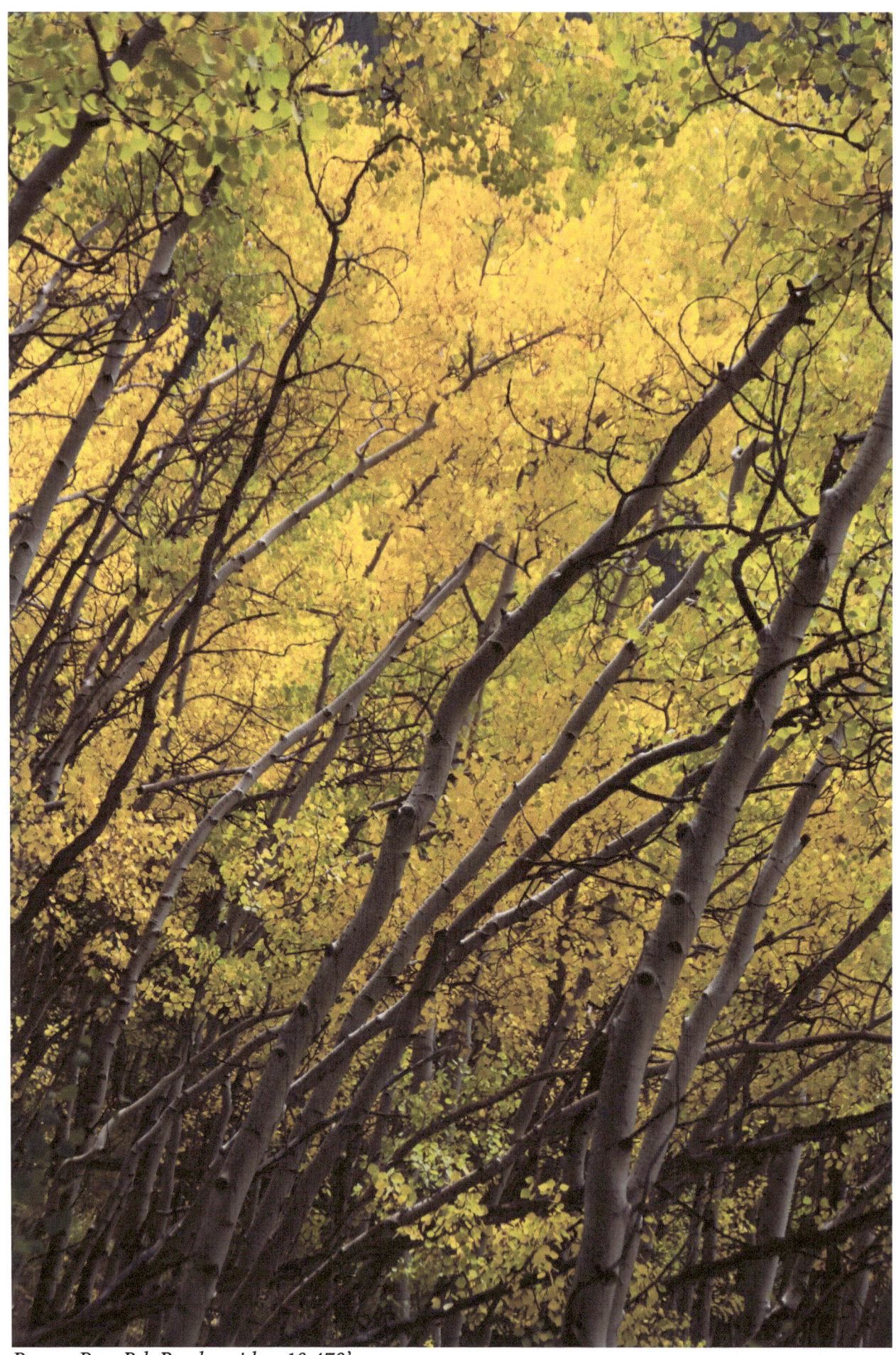

Boreas Pass Rd, Breckenridge, 10,470'

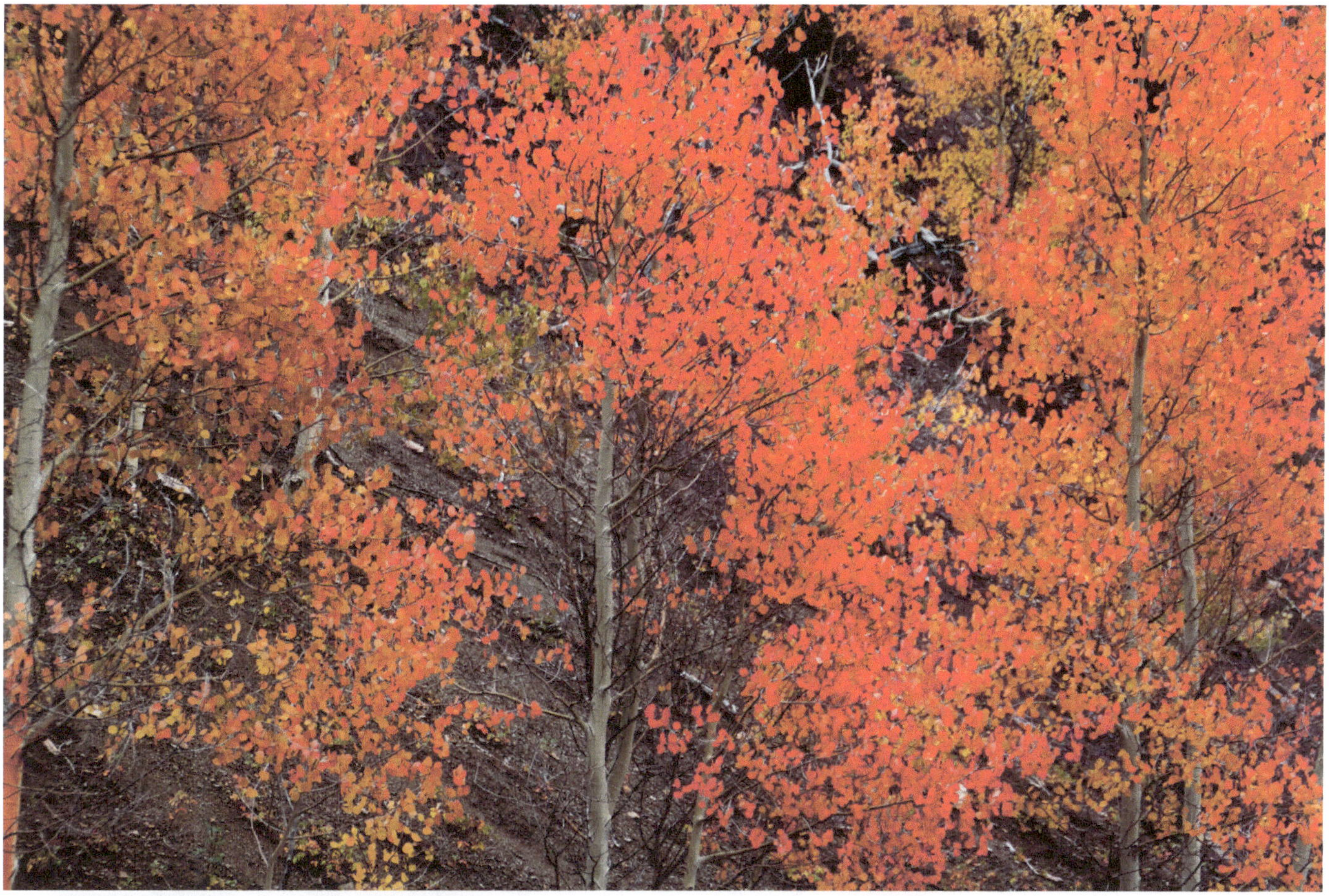

Boreas Pass Rd, Breckenridge, 10,410'

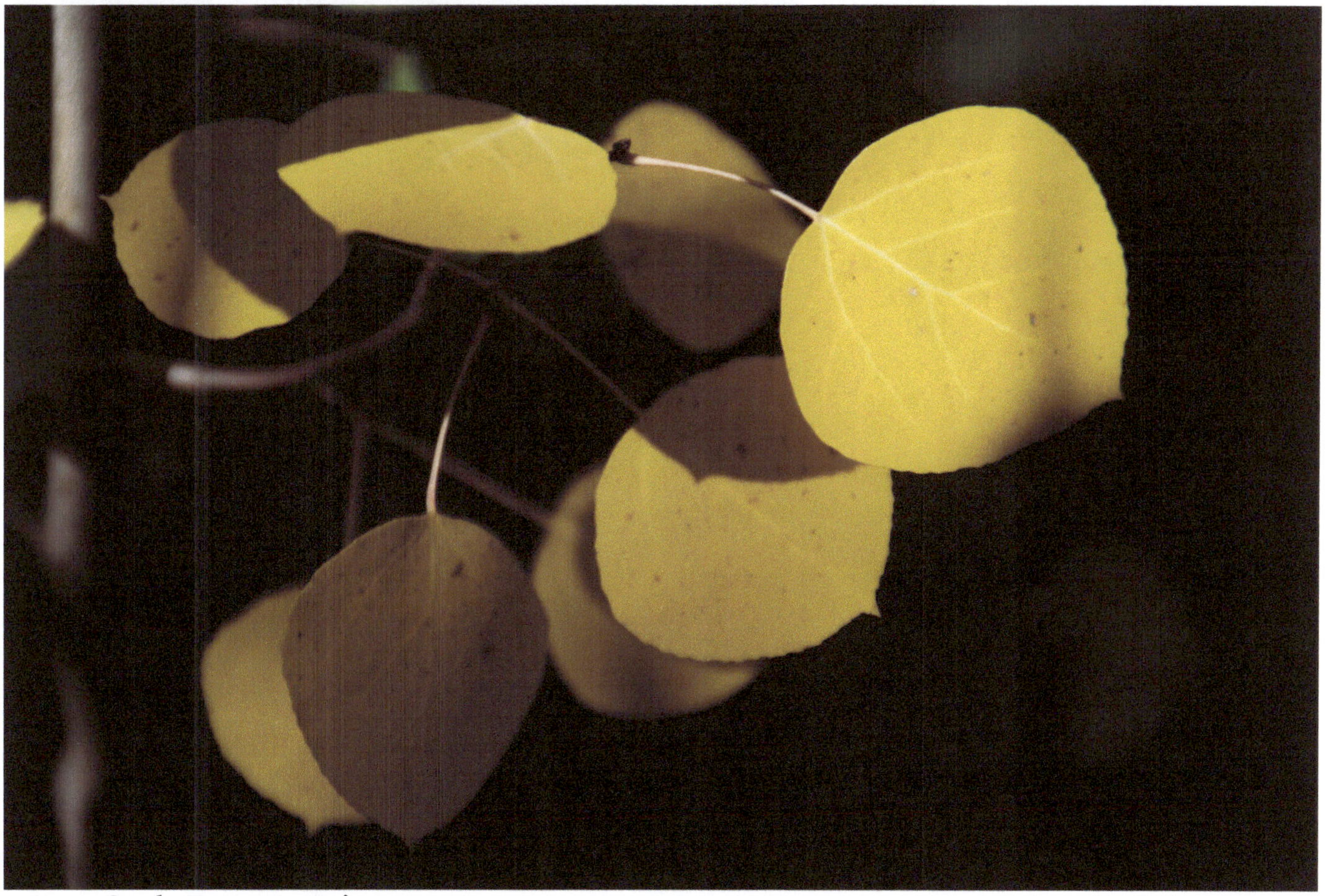

Miners Creek, Frisco, 9,120'

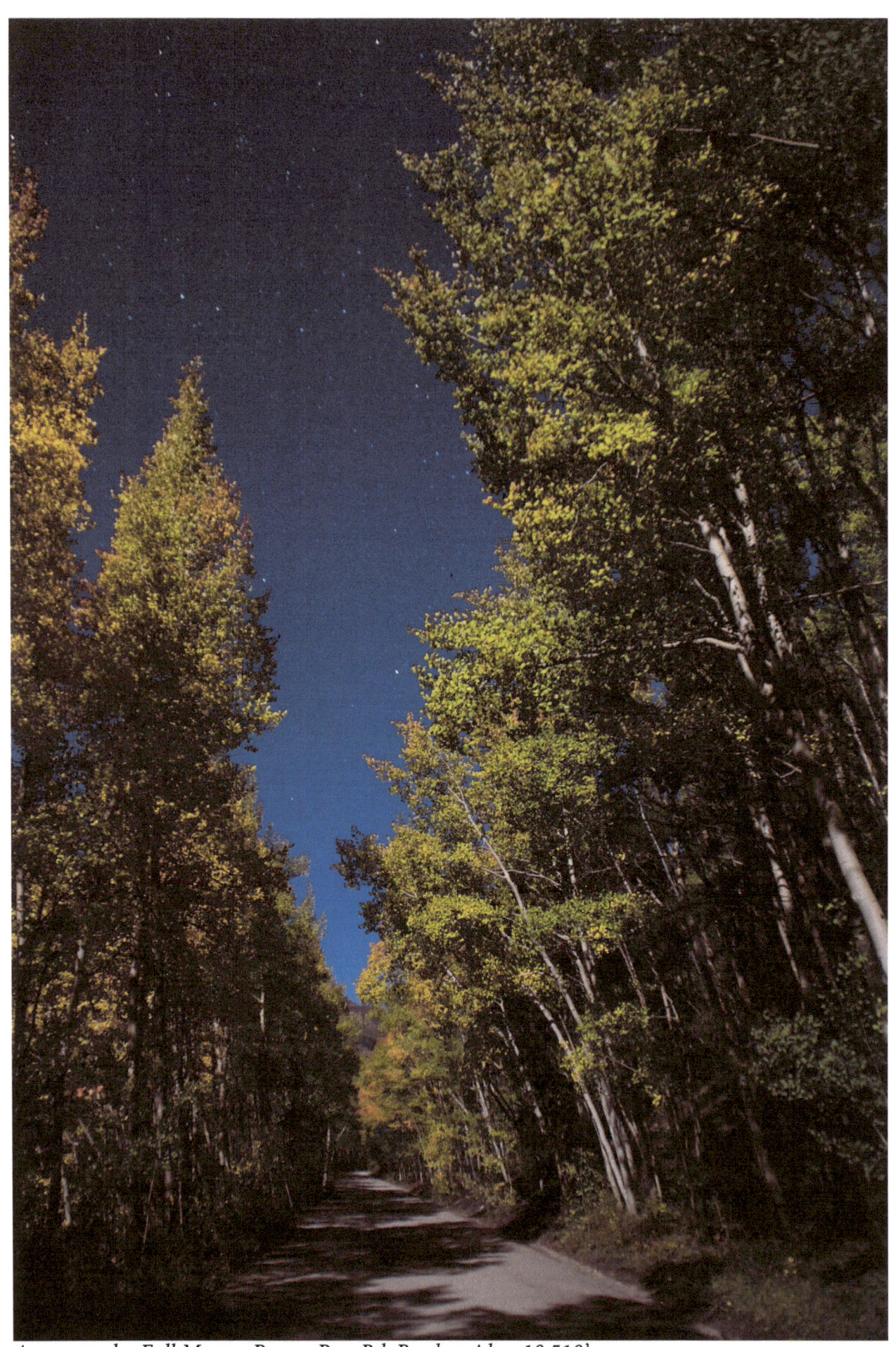

Aspens under Full Moon - Boreas Pass Rd, Breckenridge, 10,510'

Night photography of aspens is a surreal experience – and also a rare one. For starters, there is a limited window of full moon per month, along with weather concerns, angle of the moon relative to the subject, and time when the moon is up. For this season, things conspired to have a late evening photo series starting at roughly 11PM. I went up Boreas Pass Rd – which is a rather eerie dirt road passing through national forest outside of Breckenridge. I first went to the top of the pass – over 11,000 feet and above the timberline – to catch some photos of the Milky Way. Being 10 miles away from the nearest power line and cell reception in the middle of the night is odd, yet an incredibly liberating experience.

As I was taking photos, I sensed that I was not alone. I had a headlamp with me – so I turned it up to the sky to see an overly aggressive owl circling overhead. He was sizable. My headlamp served as a deflection tool – as when he went to dive bomb my head, the lamp would send him off. After a few minutes of this little exercise with this apparently displeased owl, he left. So I resumed taking pictures. I then moved into the brush to get some better views of the Mt. Baldy ridge – and again I sensed the lack of solitude. This time two owls were engaging in the aerial attack. More deflection with the headlamp – and after some minutes, they left again. As my head was buried in the camera and tripod, I heard a quiet "swish" and stood up – only to catch the wing of the second owl within 12 inches of my head. Looking around – there were now three owls – an Owl Air Force! They were all doing fighter owl maneuvers – and I was playing matador with the headlamp. If there ever was a time to leave, this was a good one.

I proceeded down the road to the stands of spruce and took some photos of the peaks in the distance. I was serenaded by the sound of a pack of howling coyotes and the mountain river rushing in the valley below. While it had an esoteric, raw beauty, the situation commands respect. I am in the dark – and any predators are more skilled than I.

Continuing down the road toward Breckenridge, I got into the aspen stands. The photos turned out dynamic – except the concern is the fact that I am now effectively in the woods, alone, at night. We have mountain lions and bears (among other things) in abundance here and while animal attacks are not common, I am a relatively defenseless, tasty steak for these guys. Proceeding down some more, I came to the area in the photo on the next page with bright orange aspens – truly a remarkable sight to behold under the serenity of a full moon. As I was taking the photos (some of which are 30 second exposures), I thought to myself "you know, I probably should get in the truck during the exposures as I just don't know what could come blasting out of that tree stand." Just then, I see the faint indications of an animal coming my way down the road. Making haste, I levitated into the truck. As this seemingly nefarious beast approached, it became evident it was a fox. He stopped within 12 inches of the door of the truck and looked at me. I had enough time to grab a crude photo with my iPhone – and when it was evident no tasty morsels were going to drop from my vehicle, he moved on. Foxes are virtually tame in Breckenridge – as I have seen then raising their young at the post office, at Starbucks, and at an indy coffee shop.

Summit County is quite remarkable at night. The Milky Way is cleanly visible to the naked eye – with a clarity I had never before seen in all of my adventures. Standing atop a ridge at over 12,000 feet looking at the stars is a surreal, spiritual experience that is impossible to forget. Night photography here is a dream at any time of year – as the moon is uncannily bright, stars amazingly clear, and foreground elements of mountains almost make photography easy when compared to operating in typical locations.

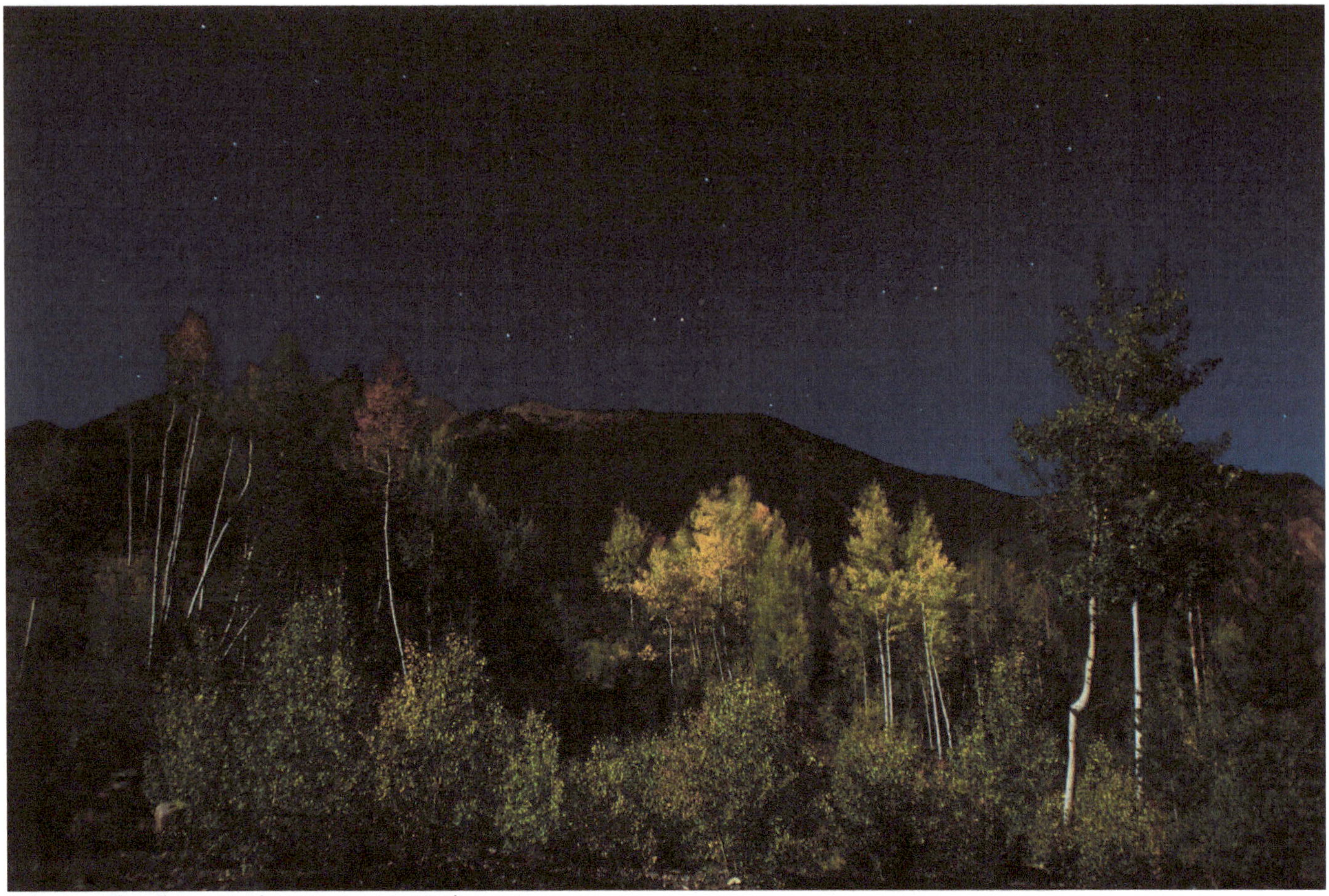

Miners Creek at Night, Frisco, 9,190'

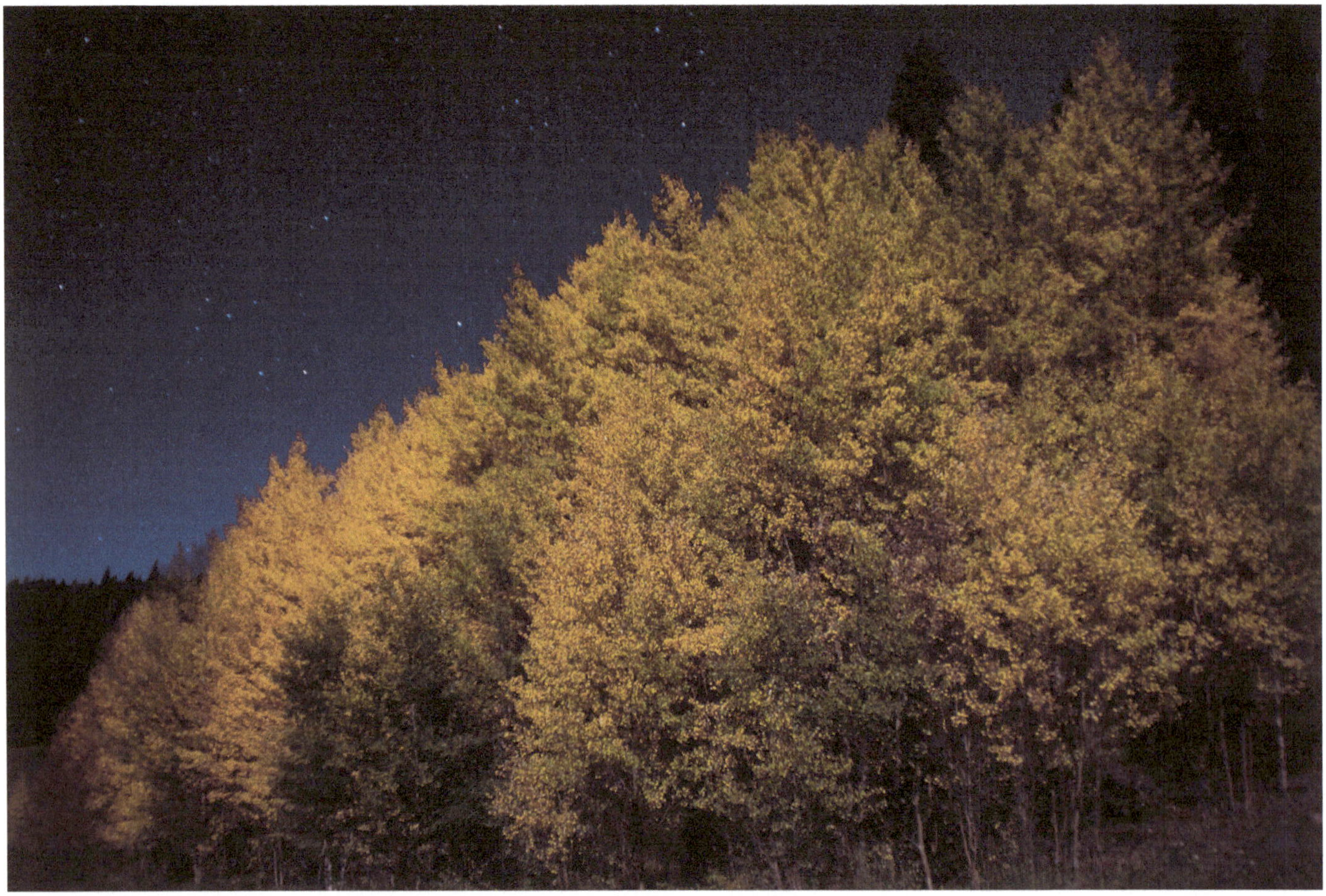

Aspens under Full Moon - Boreas Pass Rd, Breckenridge, 10,630'

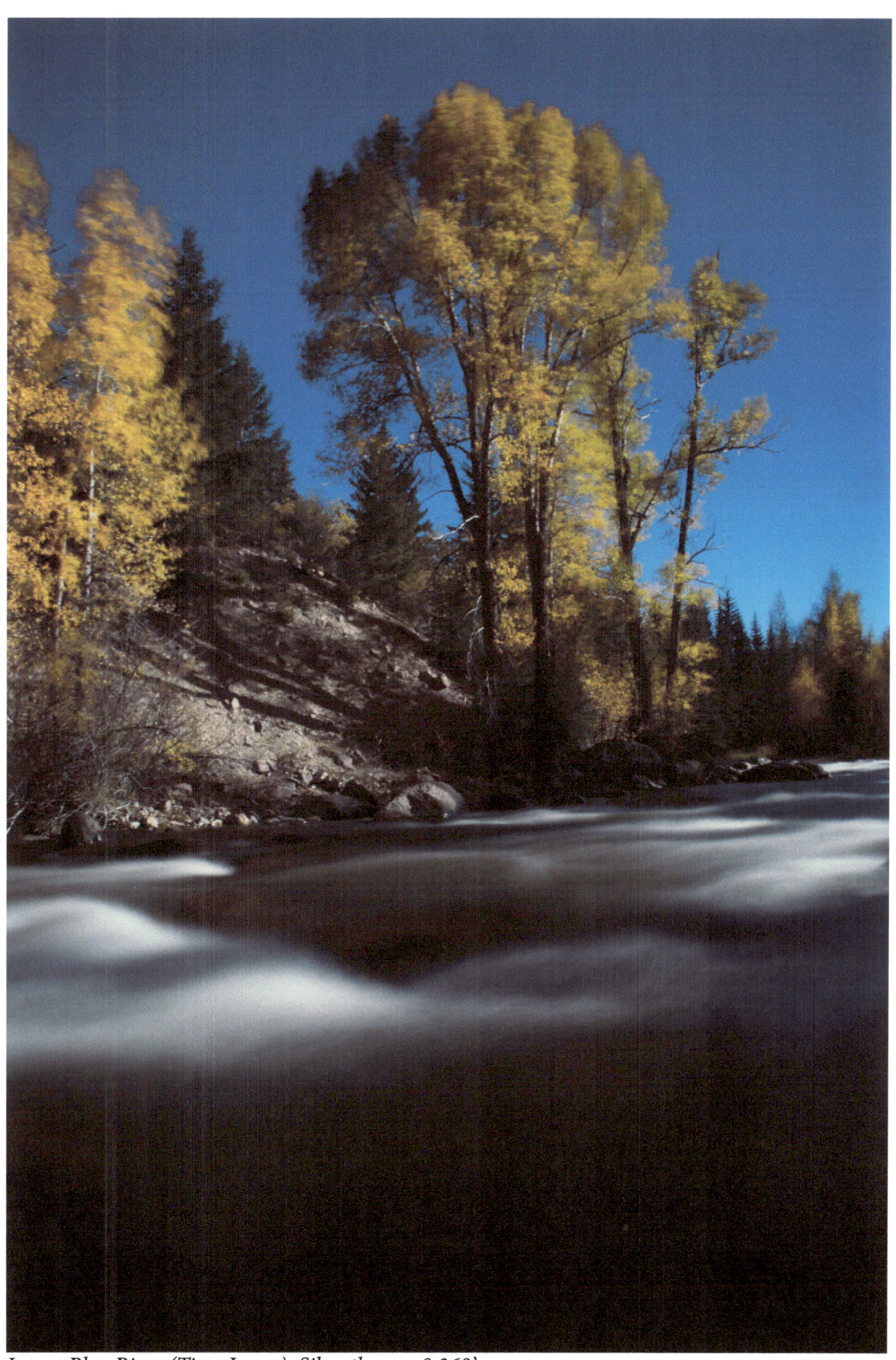

Lower Blue River (Time Lapse), Silverthorne, 8,360'

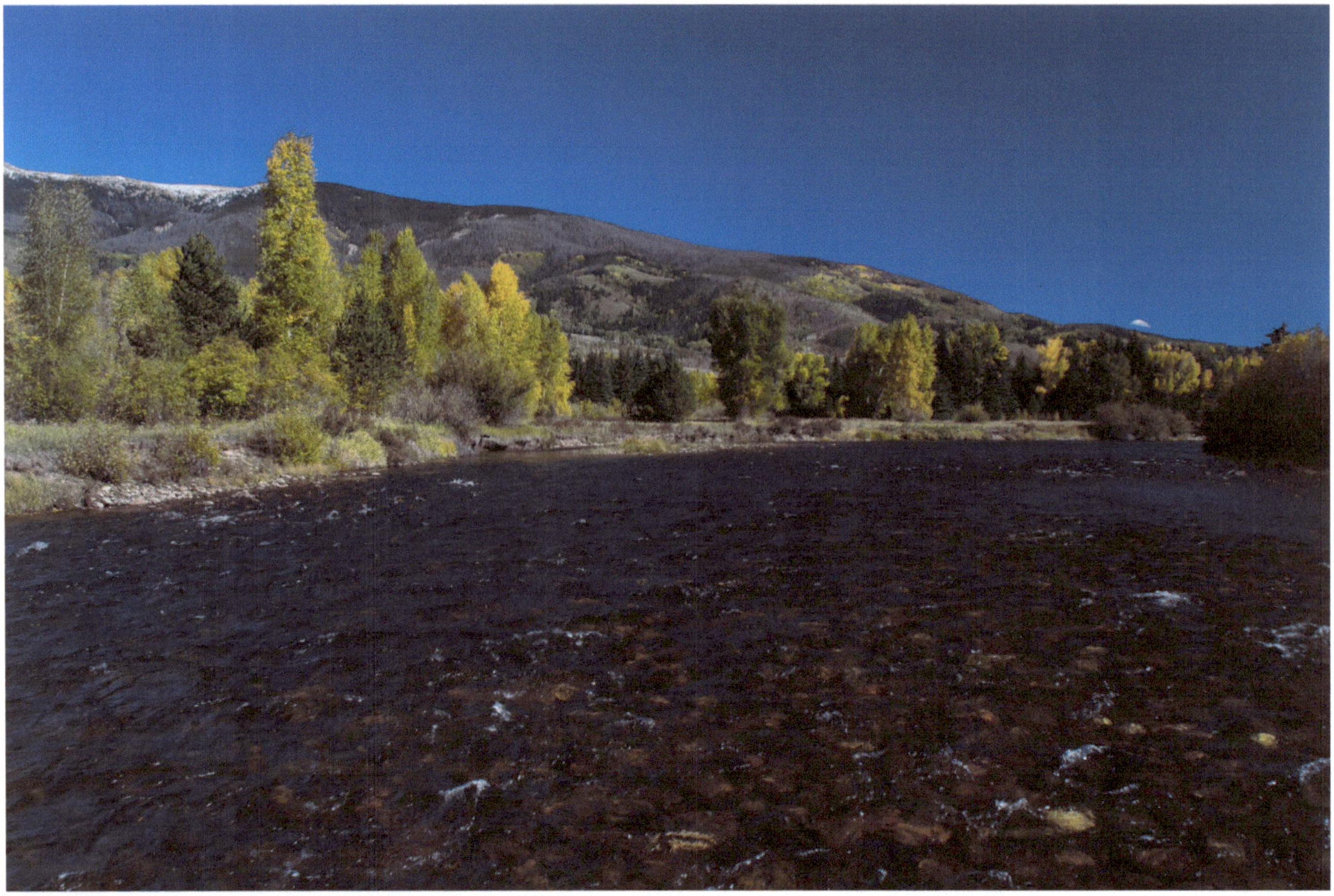

Blue River, Silverthorne, 8,510'

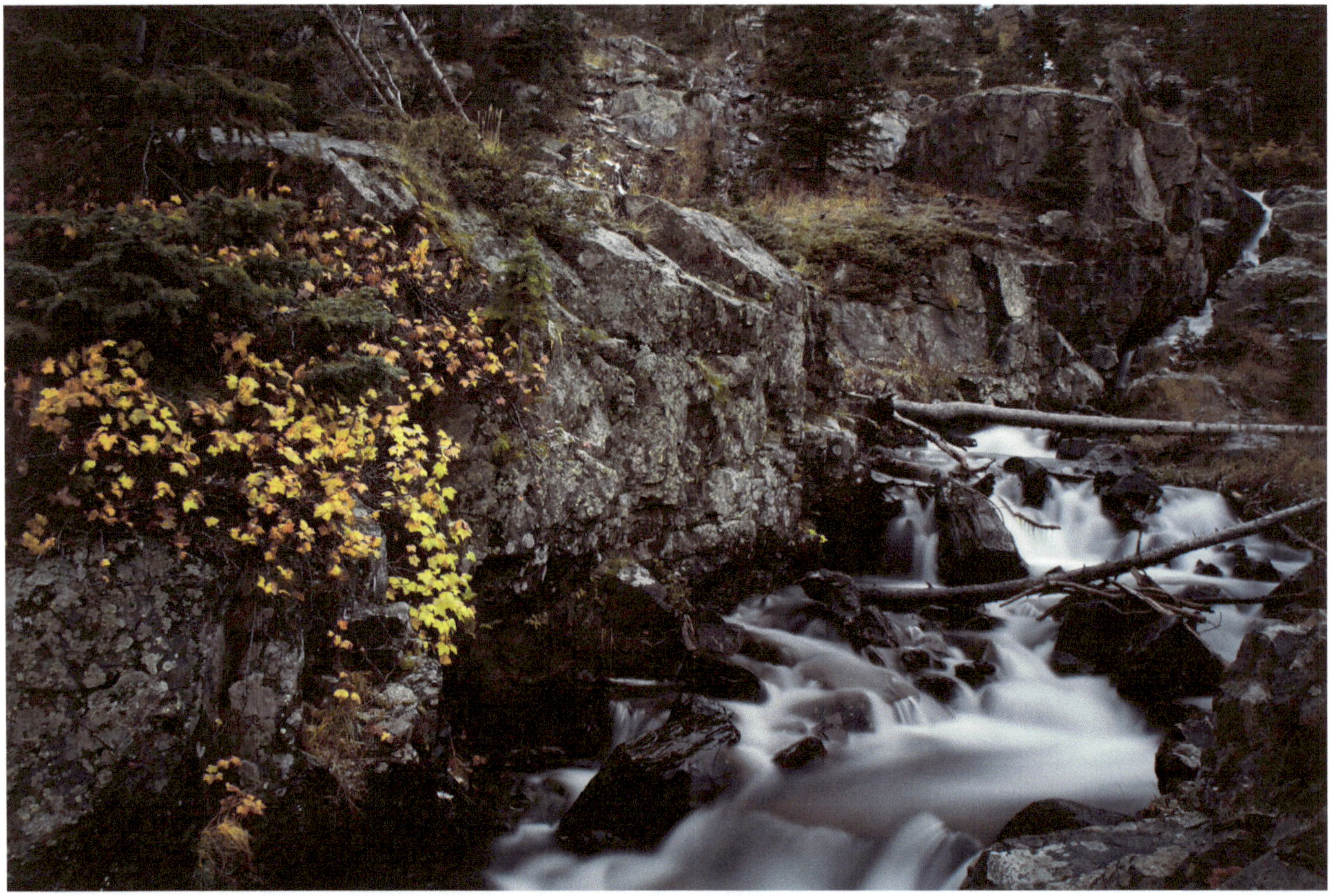

Waterfall Beneath Mohawk Lakes, Town of Blue River, 11,620'

(Bottom Left) To experience Alaska, one need not leave Colorado. Entering the foreboding domain of the timberline and mountain bowls, one can experience the rawness of the North Slope – a mere 20 minute drive from the cradle of opulence in one's own home in town. It is an important distinction that merely going to the top of a mountain is not the same as an Alaskan experience – as the top of a mountain is just raw and unforgiving in every respect possible. Entering an entire world above the timberline – yet 2,000 feet below the peaks – encircled on three sides by spires of rock – allows for an ecosystem to develop – bushes, lakes, rivers, rocks, snow fields – harsh yet not so harsh as to deny life – and one now can experience Alaska – including the feeling that you're standing 200 miles from civilization.

I had noted a stand of aspens across the valley while on Boreas Pass Rd and researched how to get there. Google Maps showed a satellite view that presented an aspen stand at timberline near some rock glaciers along what was probably a rather unforgiving 4x4 trail. Unforgiving was accurate as the "road" was just rocks – not a rocky road – just rocks. By virtue of being driven on, a pile of rocks flattened for tires to pass over – and that is about it. Some sections required some modification to pine trees to prevent scratching up the side – and others were so thin that the vehicle was pitched 10 degrees to the left just to drive down the road. The steepness and torque was intense enough to require 4x4 low – and when I was getting about to the point where I was actually considering not proceeding any further, a wider section of rocks represented a "parking lot" and the end of the road. The aspens didn't look too appealing where I had passed – and a stand of them were evident mixed amongst a rock glacier 300 feet up – so I proceeded down what looked like a trail to see what I could find.

With the rock glacier to the right, the trail proceeded through spruce trees – and immense mountains shot up to the right and left. Eventually winding to a small lake at the base of the rock glacier, the sight was something to behold. Here it is late September and it is snowing moderately with the raw sound of wind and rushing water. It looked outside exactly like scenes on nature documentaries showing animals in Siberia at the early onset of winter. Further, it felt like Siberia – alone in a vast mountain bowl with foreboding weather moving in.

I sensed the presence of a waterfall – as I had noted one in one of my photos of the mountain range from the other side. Sure enough – I encountered a cascade measured easily in the hundreds of feet. While not a sheer drop, the river cascaded down hundreds and hundreds of feet – so it had to be climbed. This was something of a challenge as it was snowing – so things were slippery – and the elevation was over 11,500 feet – which is where I personally begin to notice the lack of air. I eventually encountered the scene pictured here. The highest photo taken on land in this book – there was a delightful shrub hanging over the water – near the timberline – and while some light snow was falling.

This particular experience was quite stirring and memorable and I reflect upon it quite often since. I am remiss it was discovered just before the beginning of winter as it makes an excellent area to explore and enjoy in the summer months. My initial prejudices that Colorado was some form of water-starved, permanent drought state were completely shattered by the discovery of my second enormous waterfall – with its headwaters within 2 miles of where I was standing. For the short period of time that the alpine regions of the timberline remain warm enough to support vegetation, these regions are thick with greenery and water. The spring snowmelt feeds a sizable amount of water into the groundwater of the mountains – and that groundwater flows out during the course of the summer – supporting a version of alpine Switzerland here in Colorado. It is further remarkable that such an extreme change of terrain and surroundings is possible so close to civilization – something that does not require setting aside massive tracts of land – nor requiring a 30 mile hike to access. It is scenes like this that remind me of what life is supposed to be like.

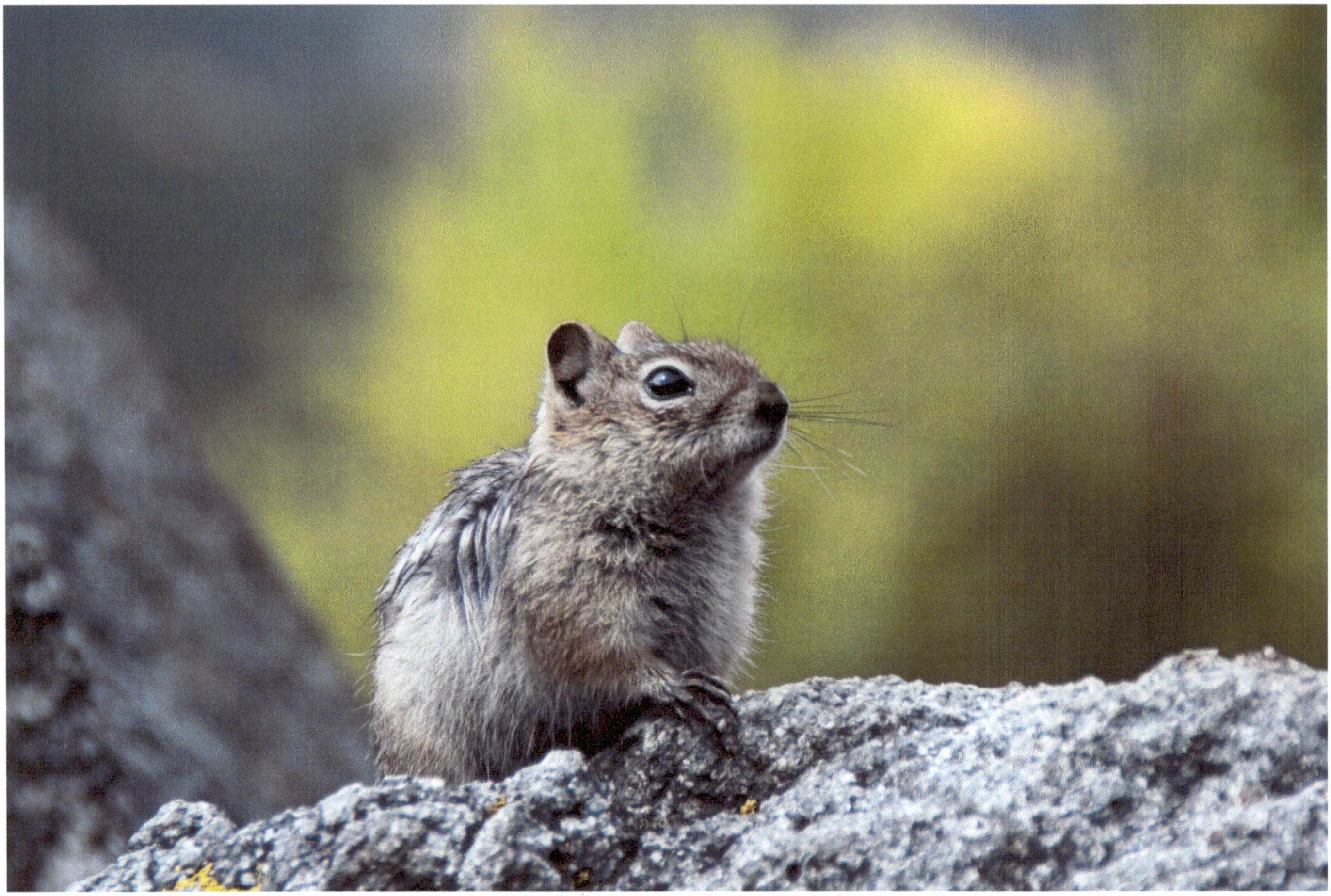

Rodent Enjoying the Aspens - Boreas Pass Rd, Breckenridge, 10,440'

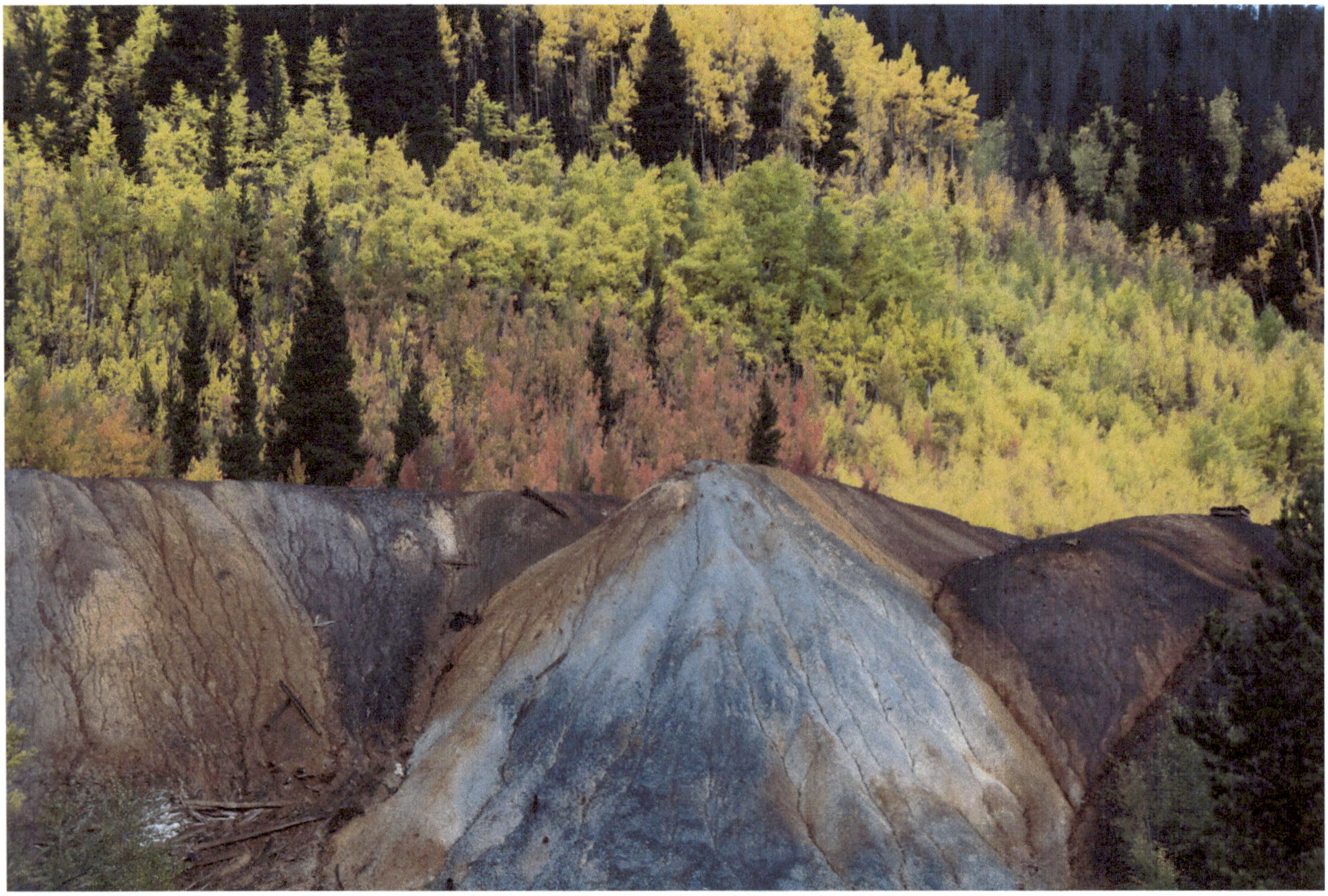

Mine Tailings Beneath Aspens - French Gulch Rd, Breckenridge, 10,000'

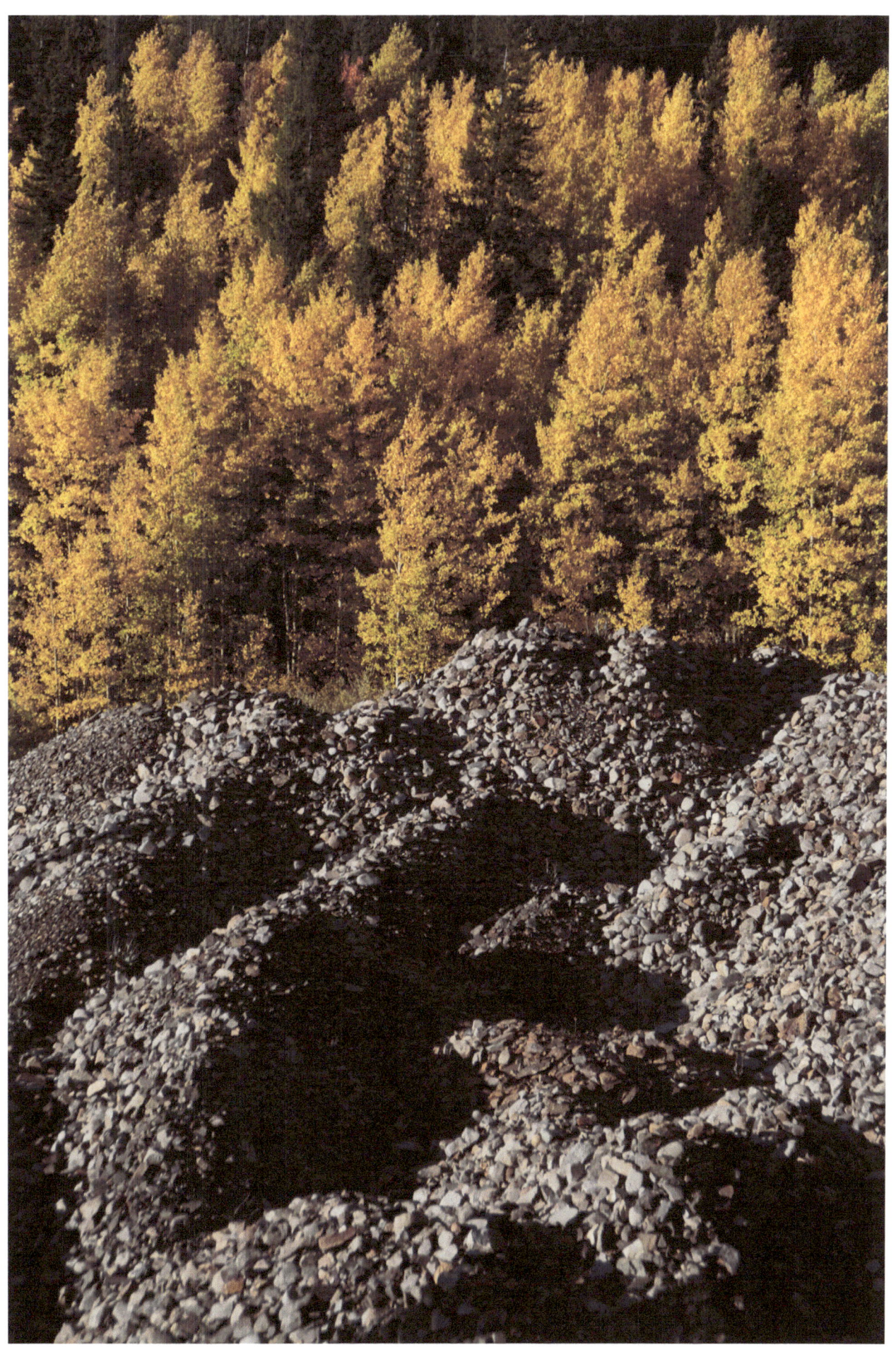

Dredge Rock Piles Beneath Aspens - French Gulch Rd, Breckenridge, 10,120'

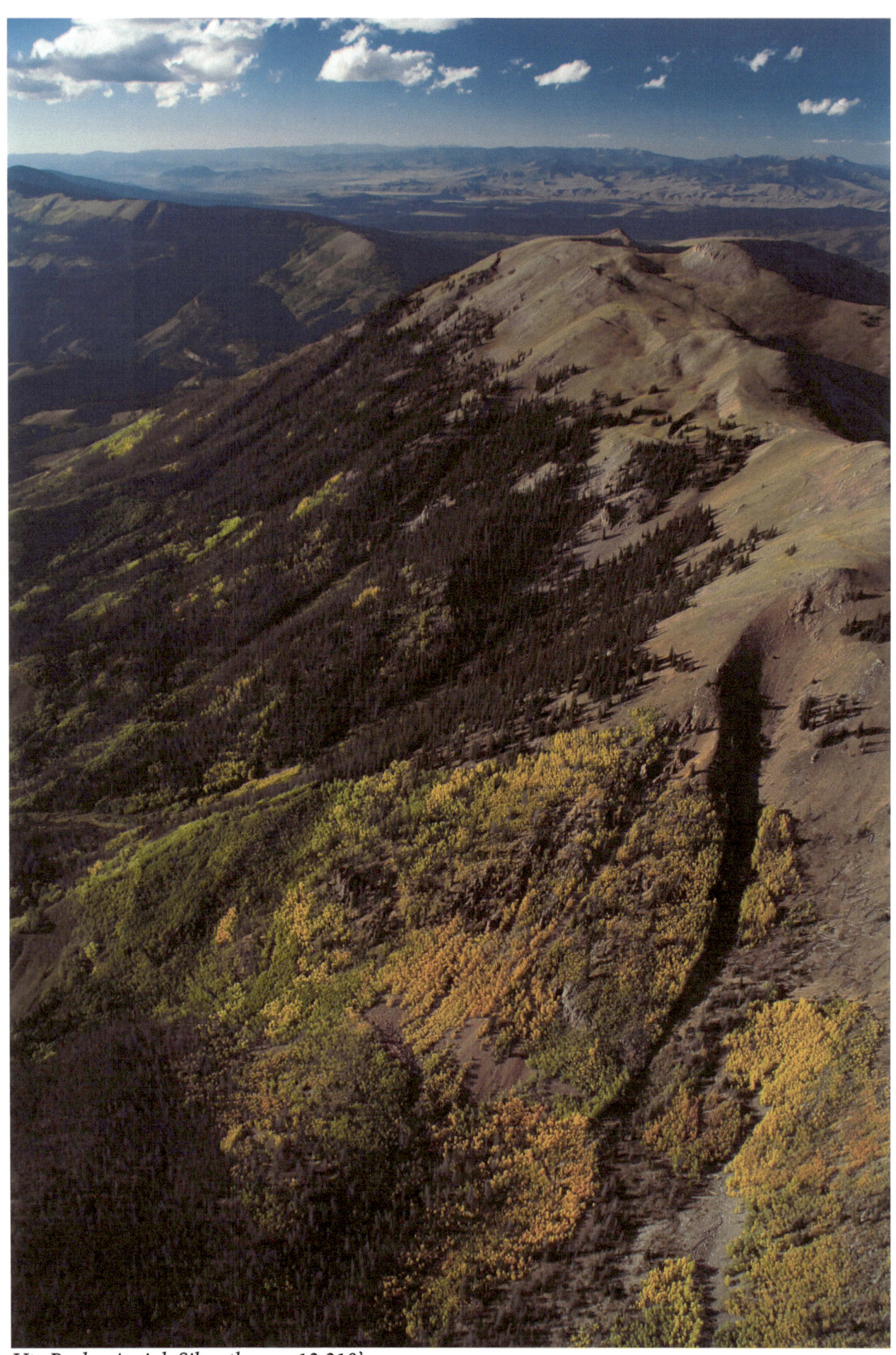

Ute Peak - Aerial, Silverthorne, 12,210'

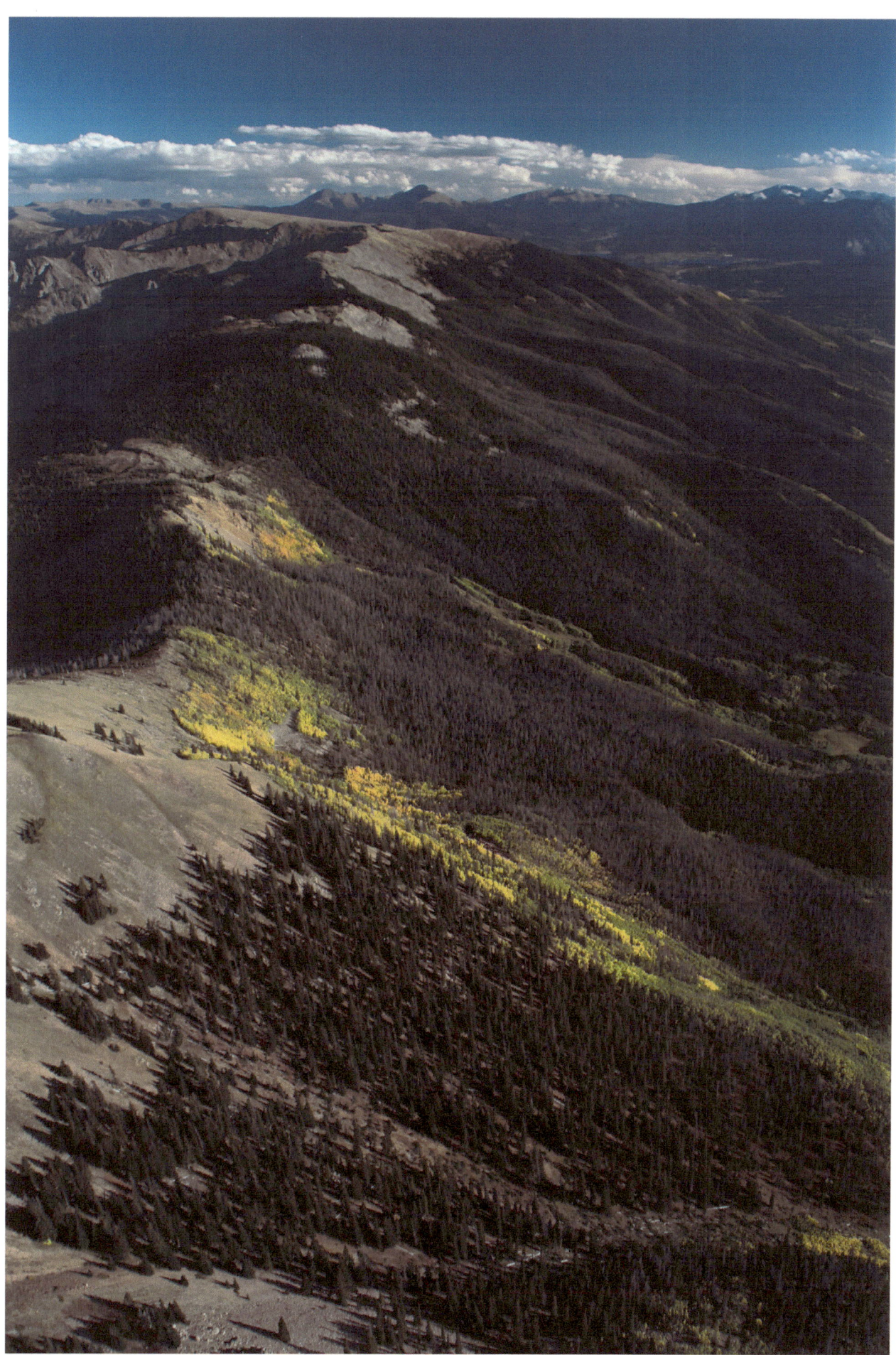

Ptarmigan Peak Wilderness - Aerial, Silverthorne

The view from the air is always a remarkable one – certainly because a person is flying – yet secondarily because things are evident from the air that are not from the ground. A person can see the entire perspective on an area – how things relate to one another – and further, aerial surveillance allows for discovering sites to see when on the ground.

For those enthused about aviation, most know that flying in the Rockies is a challenging experience. The air is much thinner and that translates into some interesting effects for airplanes. Takeoffs and landings happen faster as speed is needed to overcome lower air density. So for a sea level stall speed of 38 mph in an airplane, it may be 50 mph at 10,000 feet – yet the airspeed indicator only reads 38 mph – as 38 mph of sea-level air density is encountering the instrument. Pilots constantly have to adjust for such things. Secondly, engines have less air to use for combustion, so power reduces. In my particular case, I am able to overcome combustion issues with controlling carburetor leaning mixtures; yet, the RPM of the engine has a redline not far from full throttle – so no additional power is allowed or engine damage will result. Therefore, full RPM prop speed is turning less air molecules, effectively less engine output. If all of that isn't enough, the mountains are fickle, unpredictable beasts akin to dancing with a bear. Prevailing winds strike the peaks and do a number of things: produce rotors (rotating air) or mountain waves. A pilot really need not spend time in either – as the result is usually an acceleration of "ground meets airplane." Air, of course, cannot be seen – it can only be inferred. It takes some time to understand what the mountains are doing in general – and each day a pilot needs to figure out where the updrafts and downdrafts are for that particular day.

On the other hand, the beauty of flight in these regions is beyond spiritual. Having flown my antique airplane all over the country – from the Great Lakes to the Outer Banks, Florida, the Deep South, Midwest and Rockies – Colorado takes the cake. Not only because it is "beautiful" – because also I am able to see things that I did not know even existed from the ground. Unless a person climbs every mountain in sight, they won't see the magnitude of peaks, bowls, valleys, ridgelines, rivers and so on that exist tucked away in wilderness areas. Many of the regions here have no roads – and require quite an extraordinary amount of preparation to hike any time in the fall, winter, and spring; thus, limiting the most avid of hikers to a small section of the year. To make matters worse, summer thunderstorms are synonymous with the Apocalypse – so hiking is often limited to period from sunrise to 1PM.

Flying tosses the shackles of meteorological imprisonment to the wind and allows a person to view immense stands of wilderness monuments in a short period of time. Ten years of arduous hiking can be accomplished in a day. The value is not simply that one can see "a lot" – it goes far deeper than that. The magnitude of the region here in the Rockies is climactic – and the value of seeing the details of the area go beyond the pretty pictures. I find that when I climb a peak outside of Breckenridge or Frisco – one of the many peaks sneering at me all day as I drive past them – I have an intimate understanding of what makes the place tick: why thinks look and act the way that they do, why snow piles up on certain cornices, why certain areas avalanche each winter, why animals do the things they do in their habitats. The irony of living here is that we are all valley dwellers – relegated to lodge pole and spruce pine forests in the relative flat lands down at 9,000 to 11,000 feet. It is another world above those heights – one we don't spend time in unless we go there – and one where there is no human development. Thus, we can spend a lifetime *looking* at something and never *experiencing* it. Flying adds another dimension to experiencing the details of what lies over the next hill.

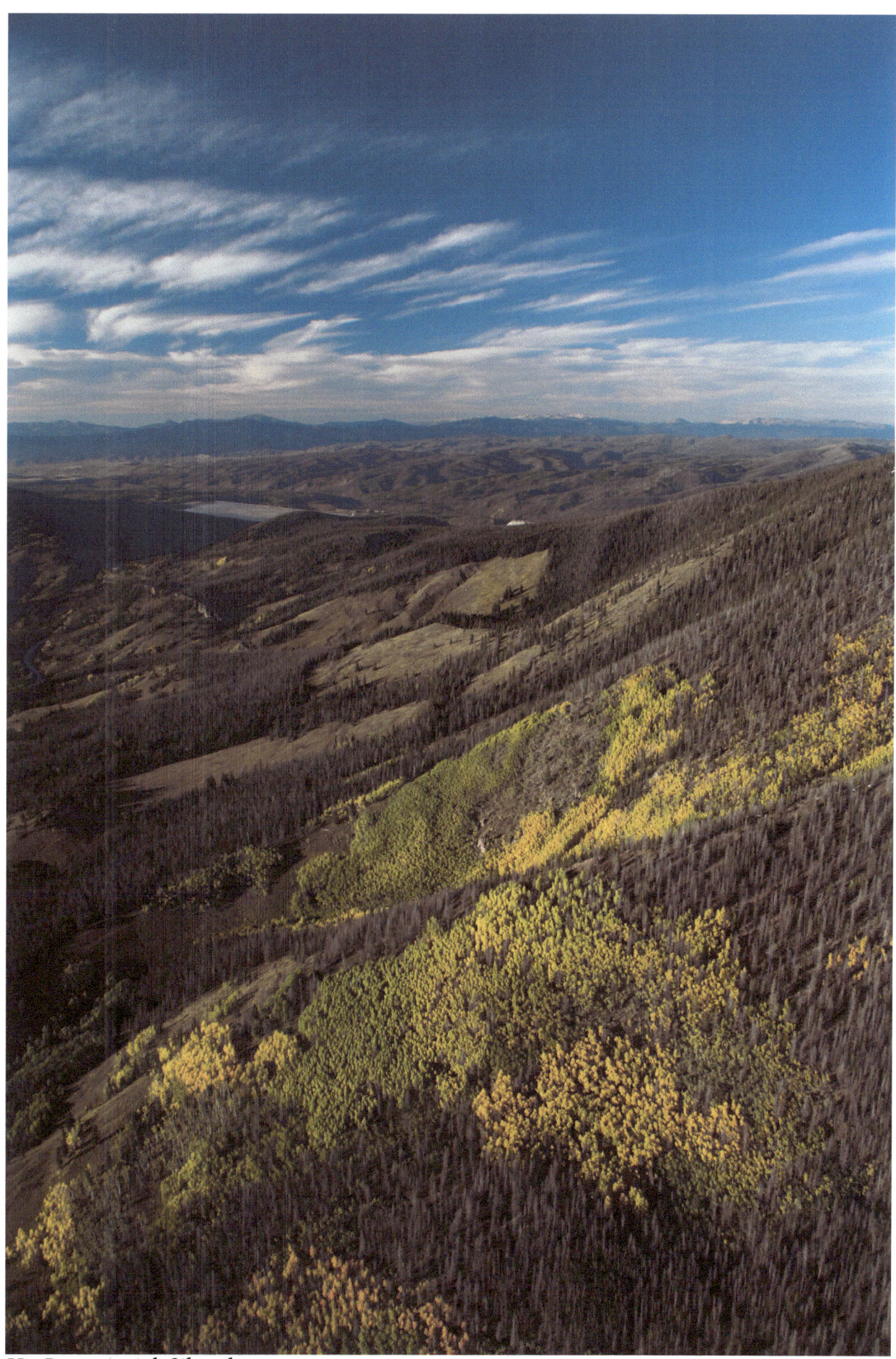

Ute Pass - Aerial, Silverthorne

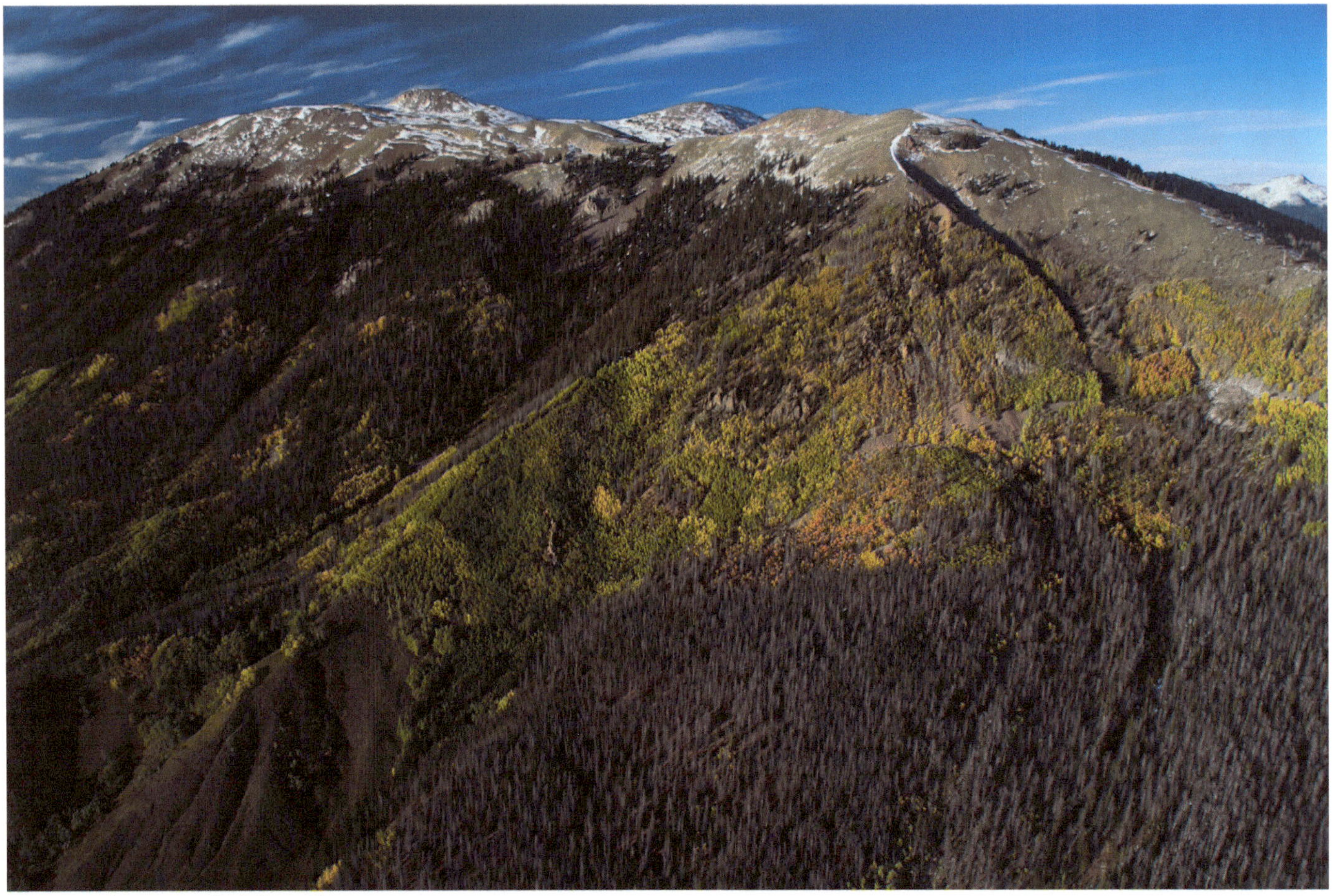

Ute Peak - Aerial, Silverthorne

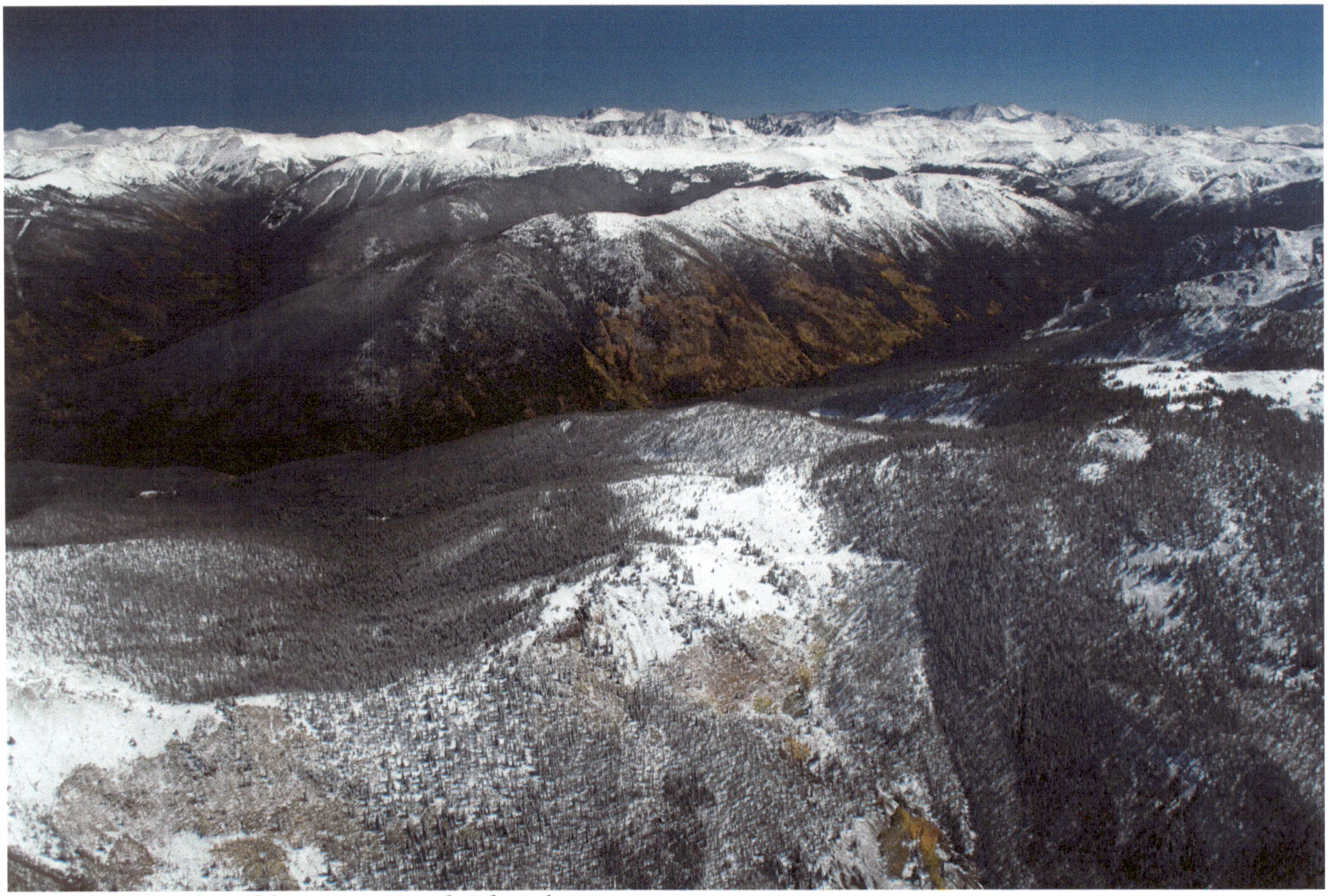

Ptarmigan Peak Wilderness - Aerial, Silverthorne

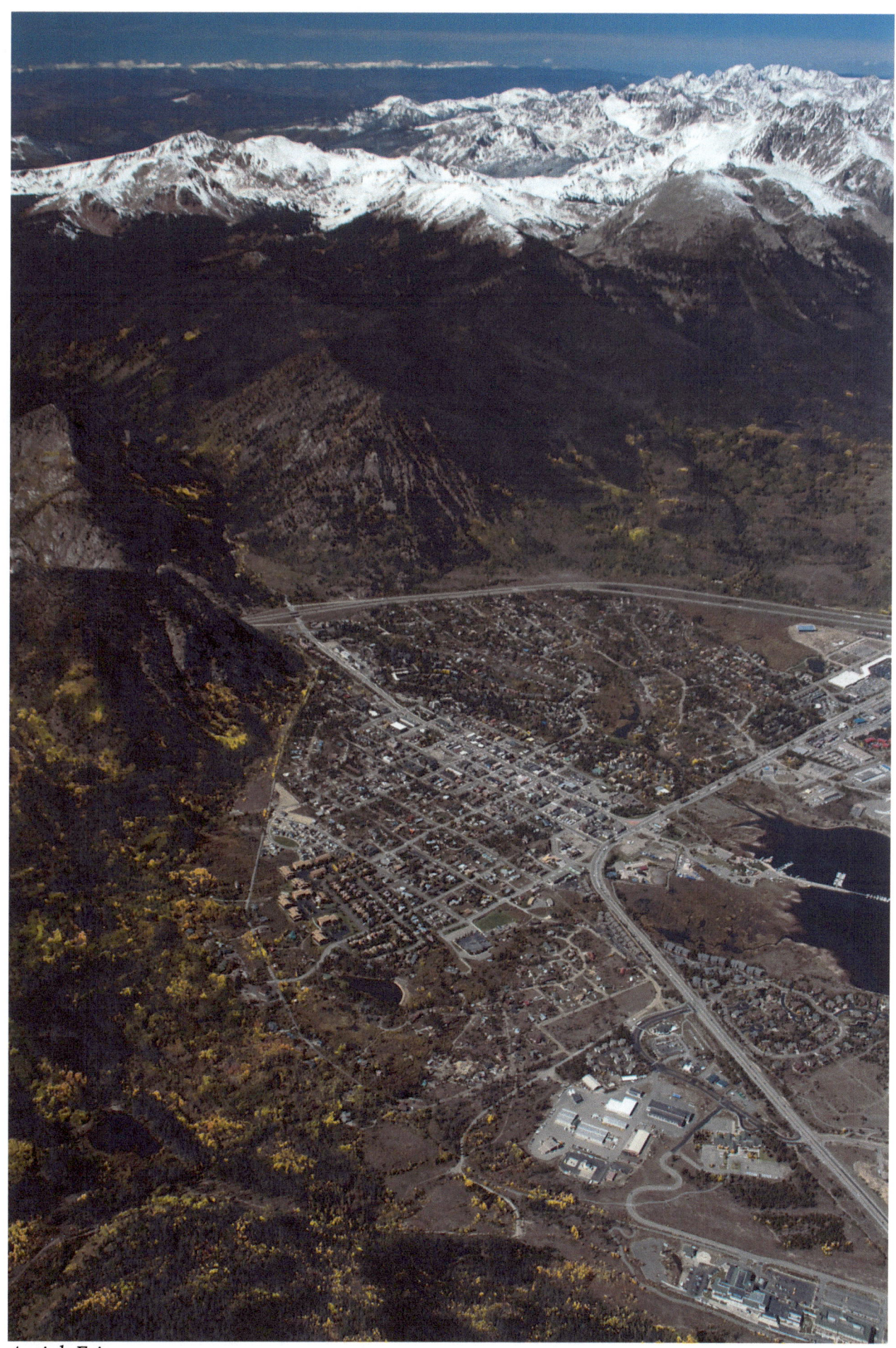

Aerial, Frisco

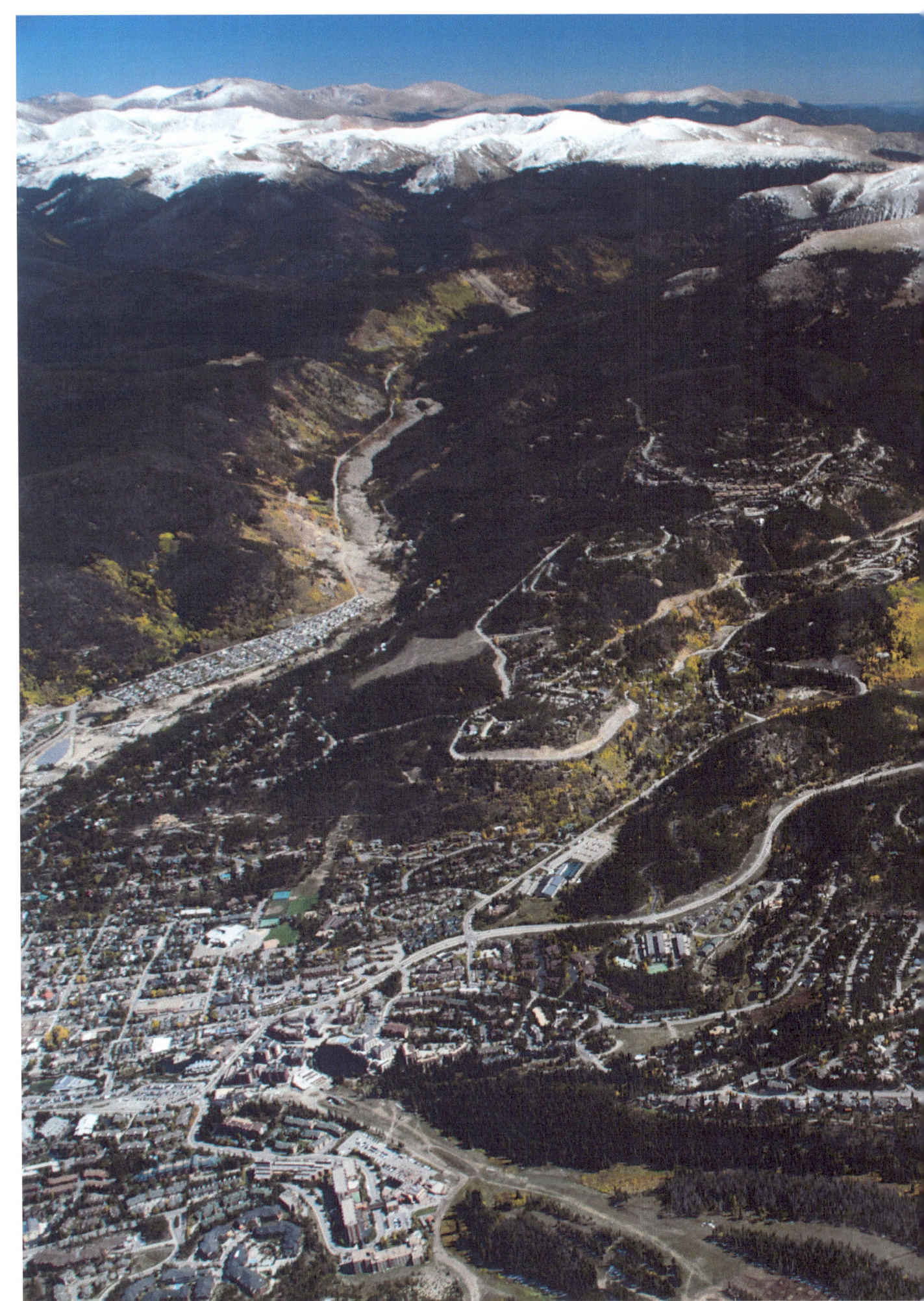

Village (Lower Left), French Gulch Rd (Middle Left), Boreas Pass Rd (Center Right) - Aerial, Breckenridge

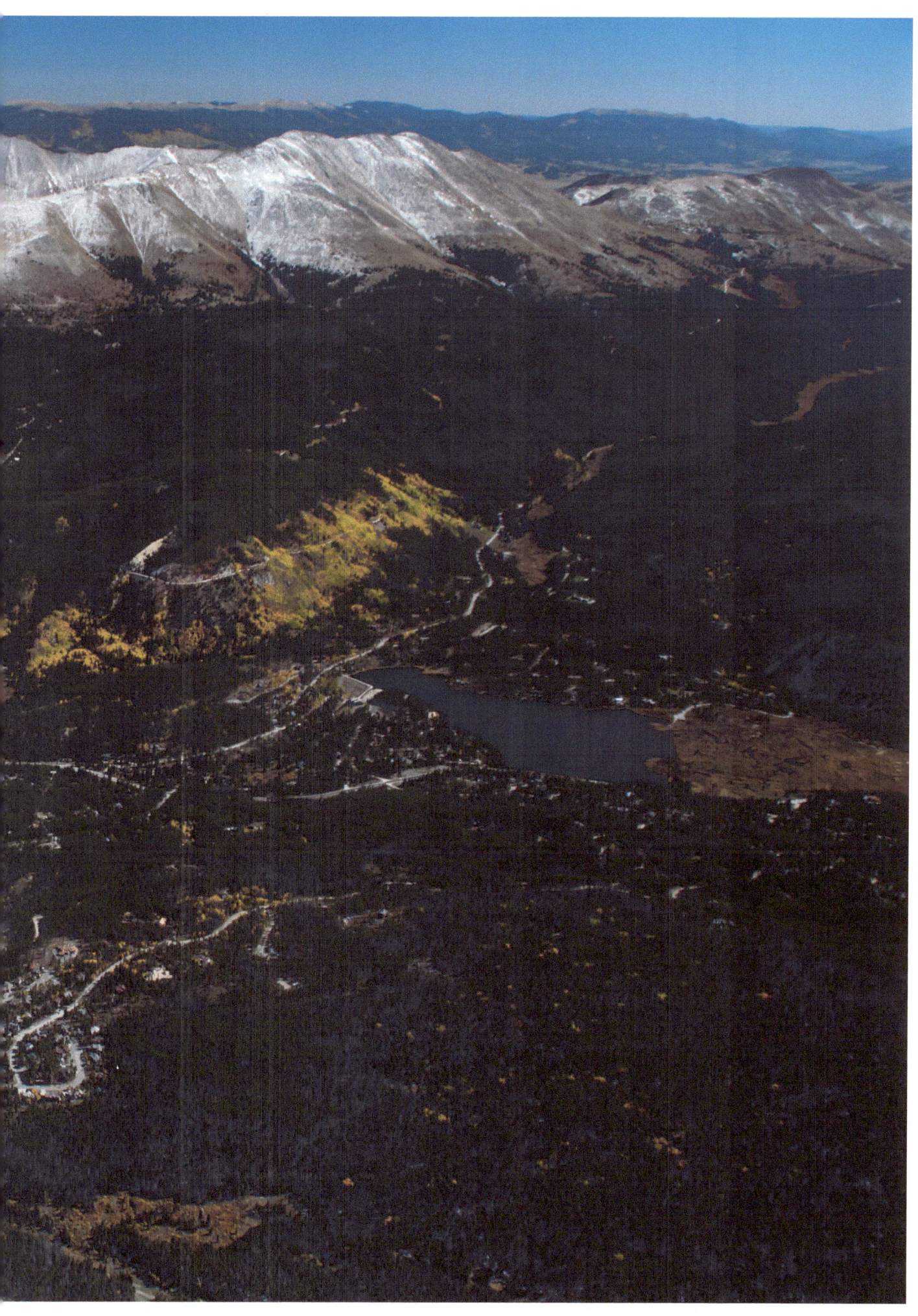

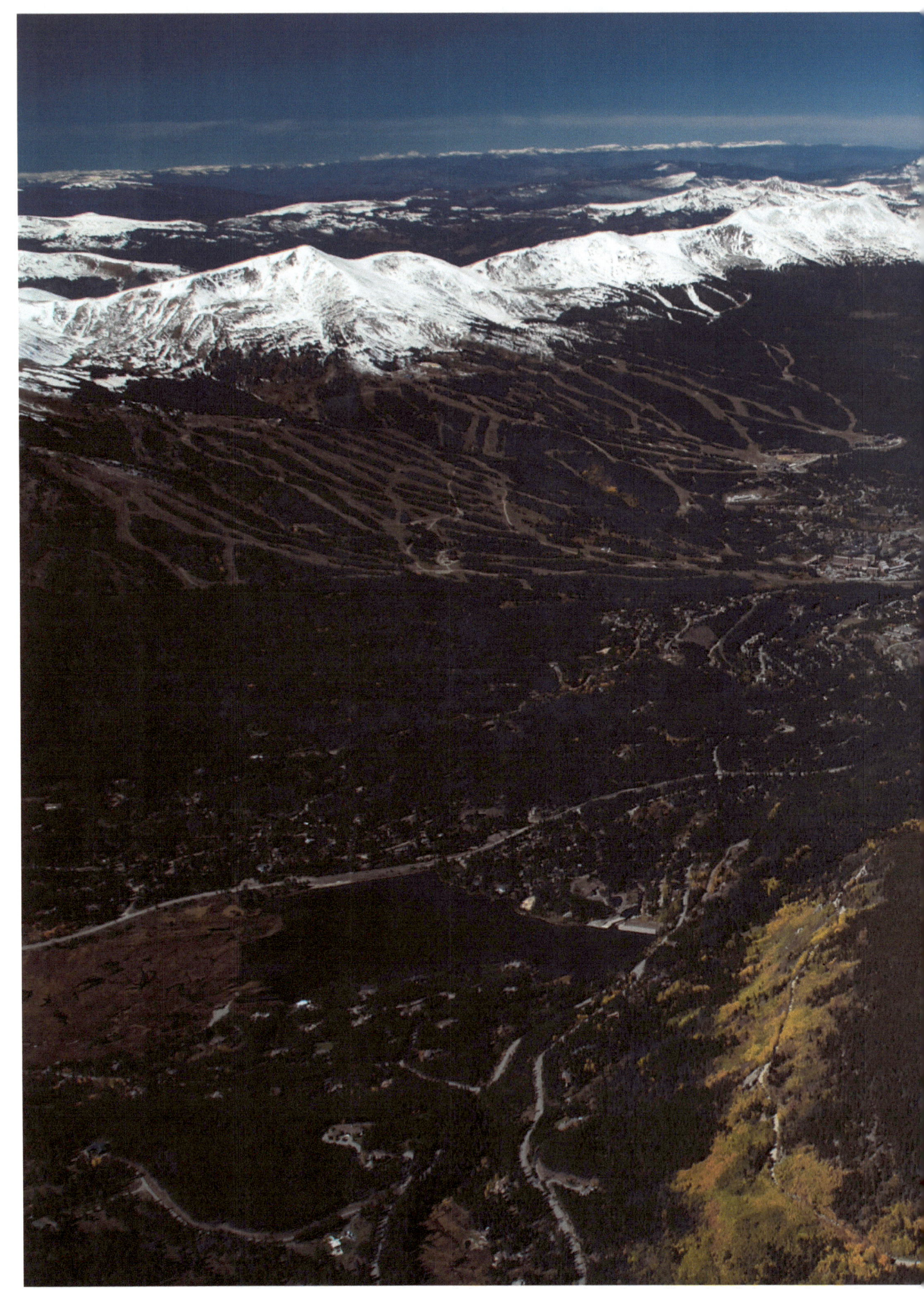

Village (Center), Resort (Left Center), Boreas Pass Rd (Lower Center), Lake Dillon (Right), Breckenridge

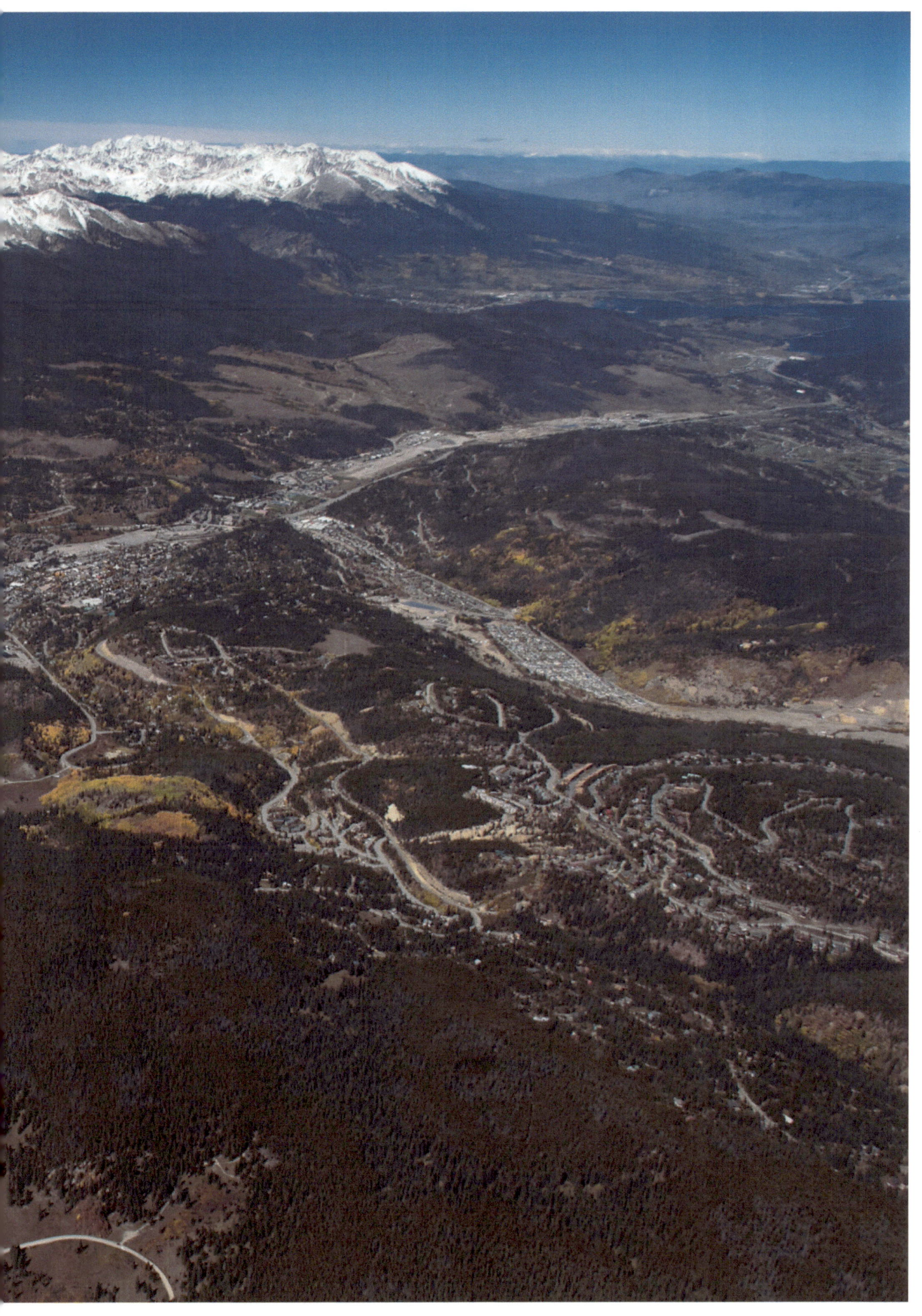

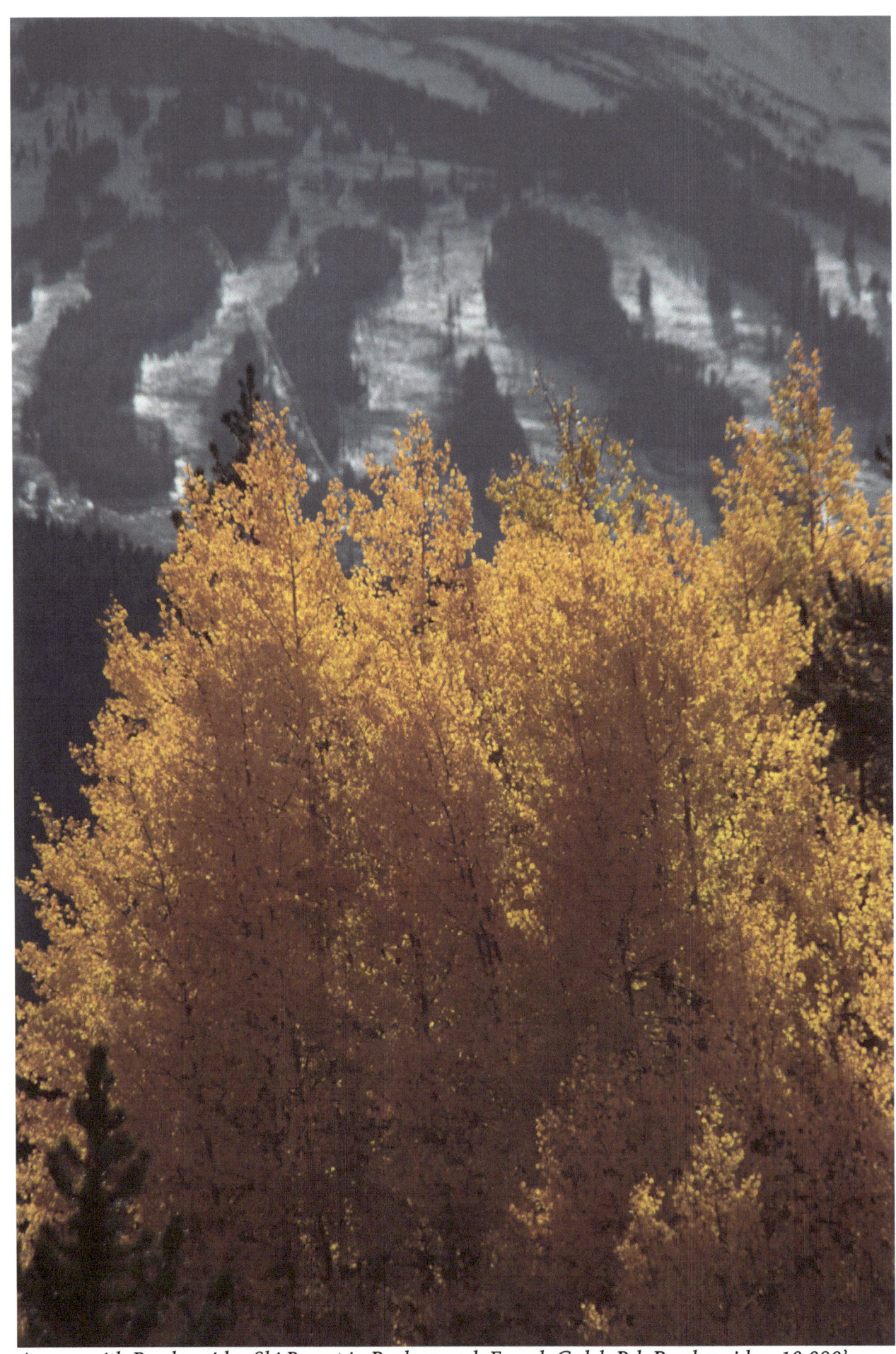

Aspens with Breckenridge Ski Resort in Background, French Gulch Rd, Breckenridge, 10,080'

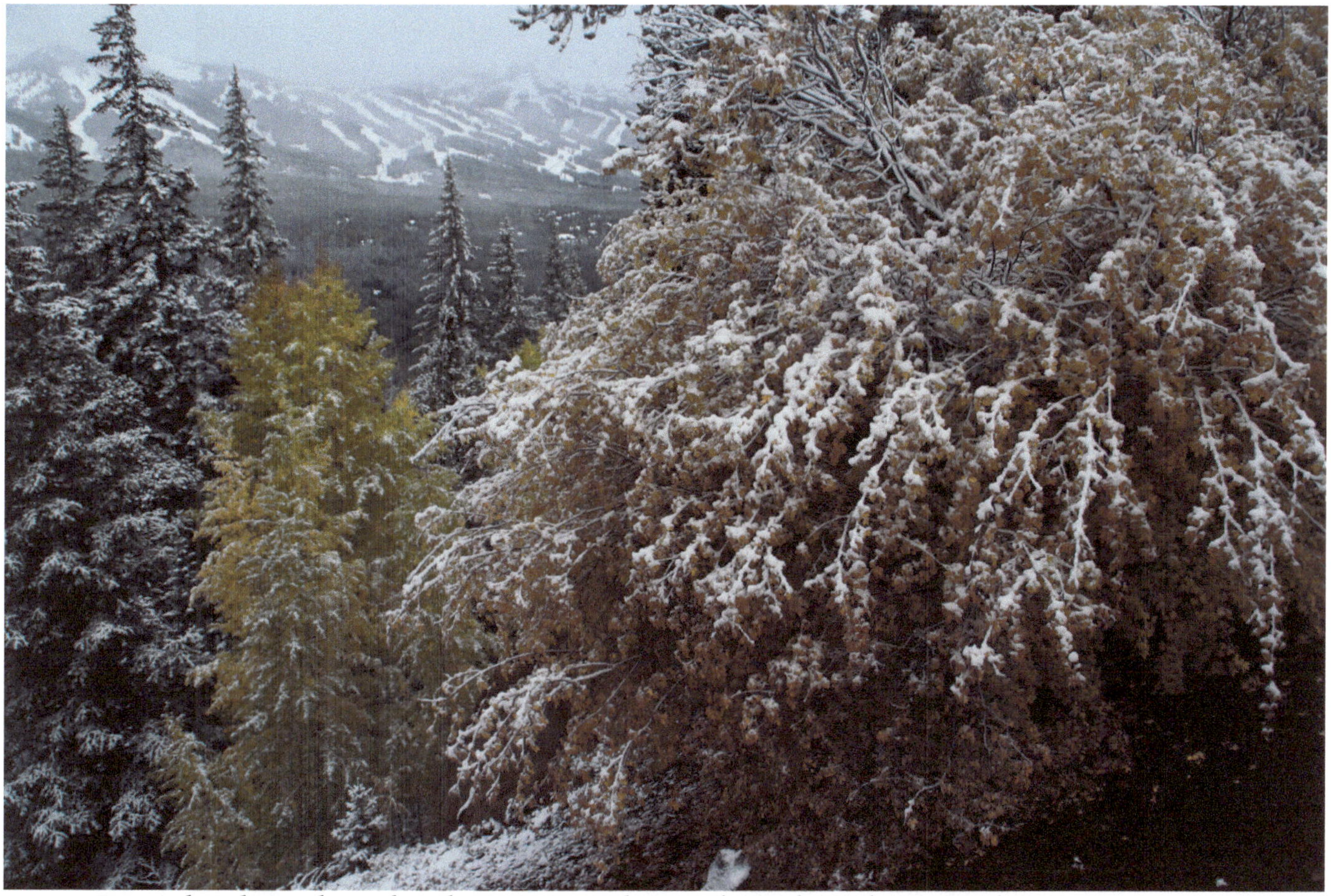

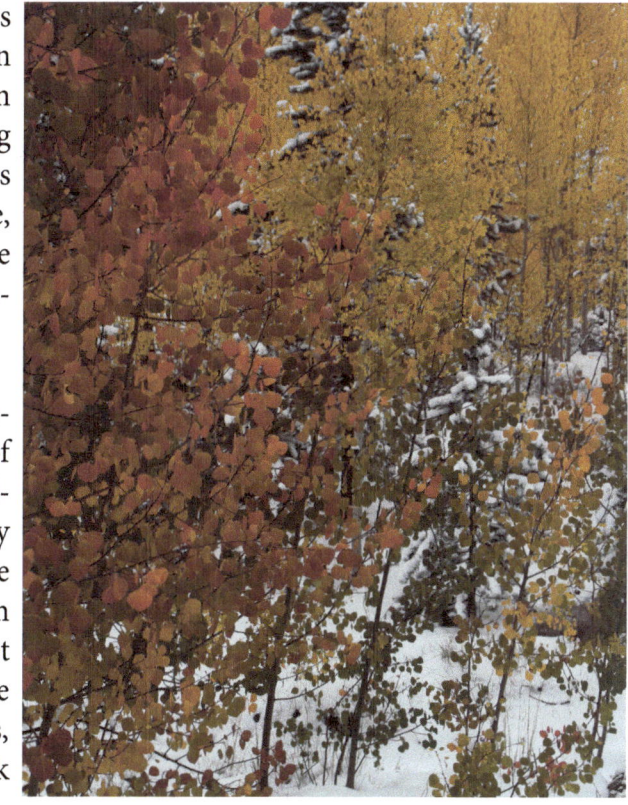

Boreas Pass Rd with Breckenridge Ski Area in Background, Breckenridge, 10,400'

The onset of winter in the high Rockies is incredibly quick by anyone's standard – yet at the same time affords a progressive warning. There is brimming excitement the first time snow shows up on the peaks (this year, it was August 7). As continuing weather comes through, the snow slowly creeps down – and melting cycles in between take longer and melt less of the snow. With autumn in explosive color, the snow creeps incredibly close – flirting with the current color bloom. The next storm after that arrives and drops snow on the aspens in color. In this particular case, the next series of photos shows the snow as it accumulated one morning from 10,000 feet and higher – and mysteriously non-existent in the village 400 feet below.

Snow spells the end of aspen color roughly two days after accumulating on the leaves. They do not fall under the weight of the snow; rather, they remain in full color for the day. The following day, the colors begin to show a dullness to them and by the second day, the leaves have turned brown or fallen. On one hand, the experience is unlike the East Coast as the leaves can bear the snow. On the other, we go from full peak to the onset of winter in a matter of 36 hours. Interestingly, this experience only occurs where the leaves have changed. At lower altitudes, if the leaves are green or have not received snow yet, the peak may continue in a valley with a hill barren of its color.

Snow, Green Leaves, Fall Color, Frisco, 9,120'

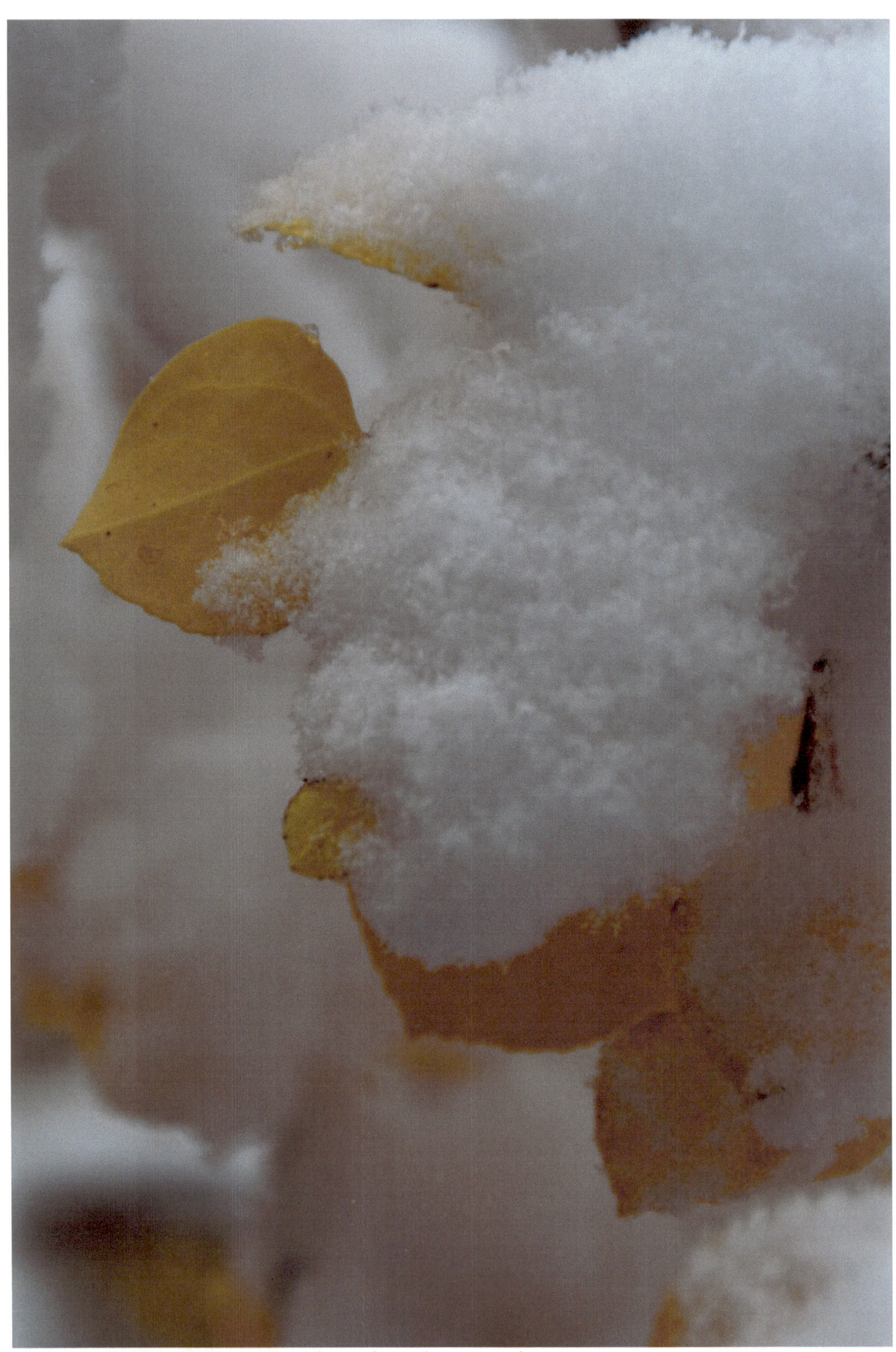

Aspens with Snow, Boreas Pass Rd, Breckenridge, 10,630'

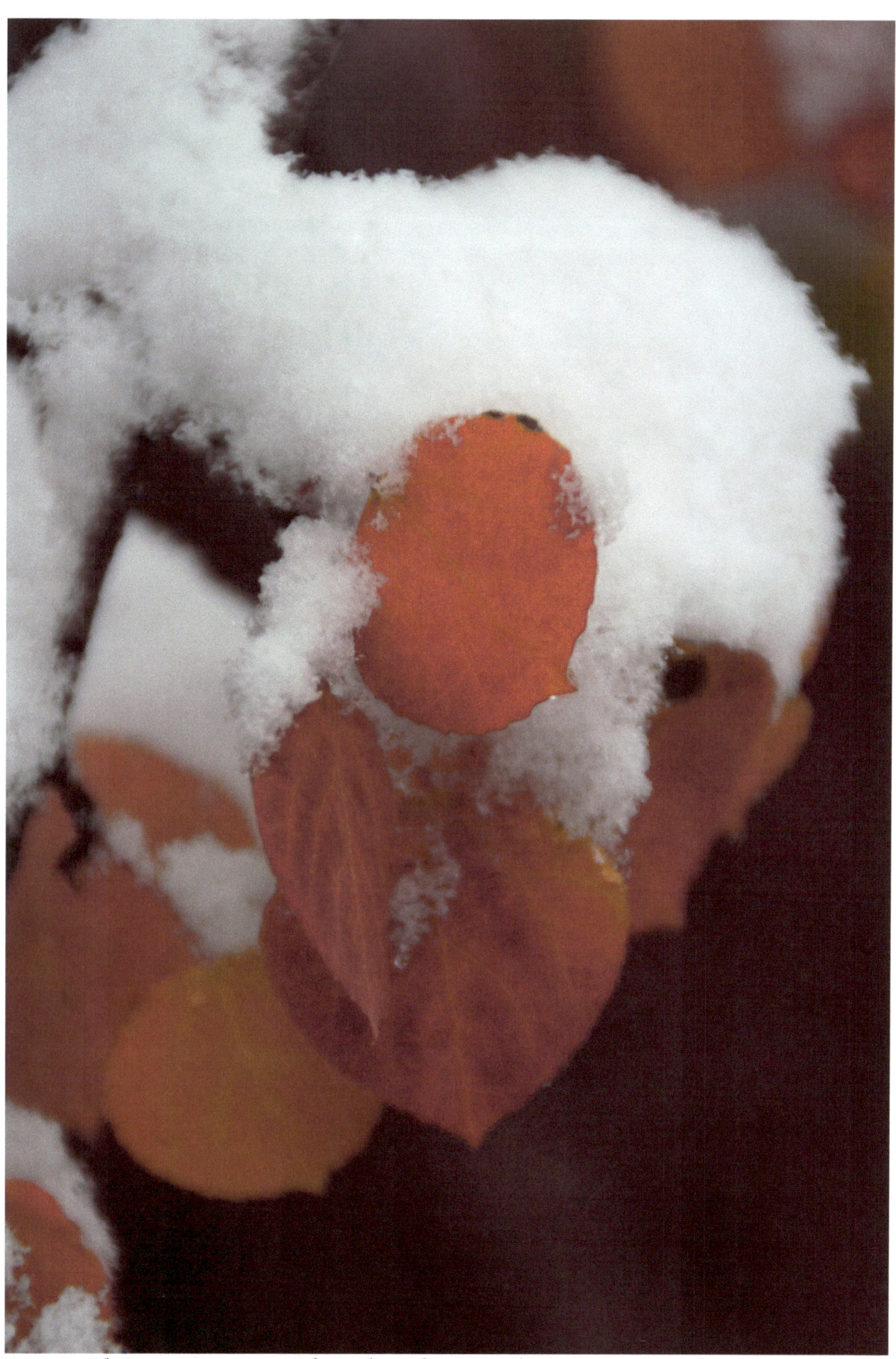

Aspens with Snow, Boreas Pass Rd, Breckenridge, 10,820'

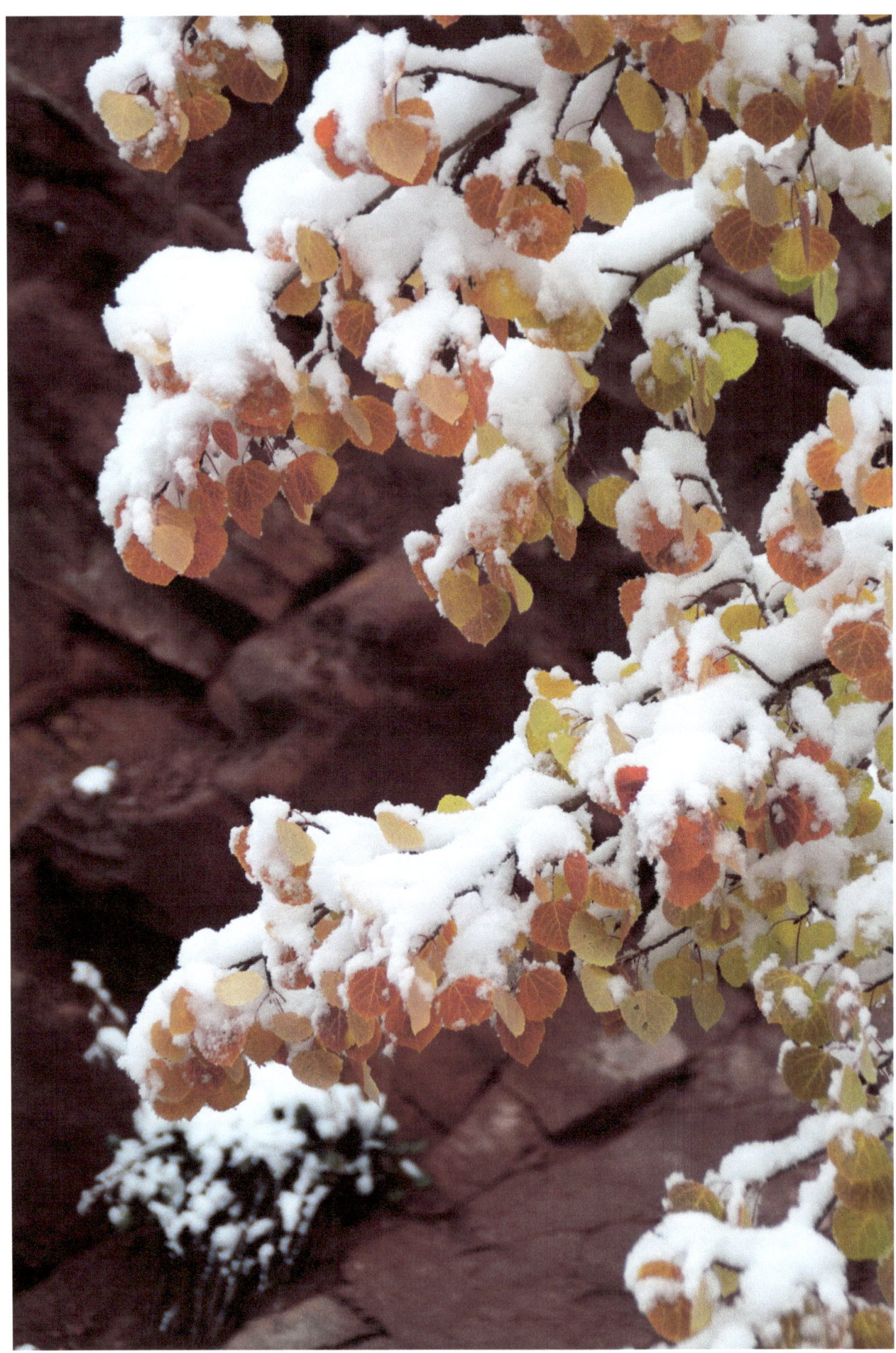

Aspens with Snow, Boreas Pass Rd, Breckenridge, 10,820'

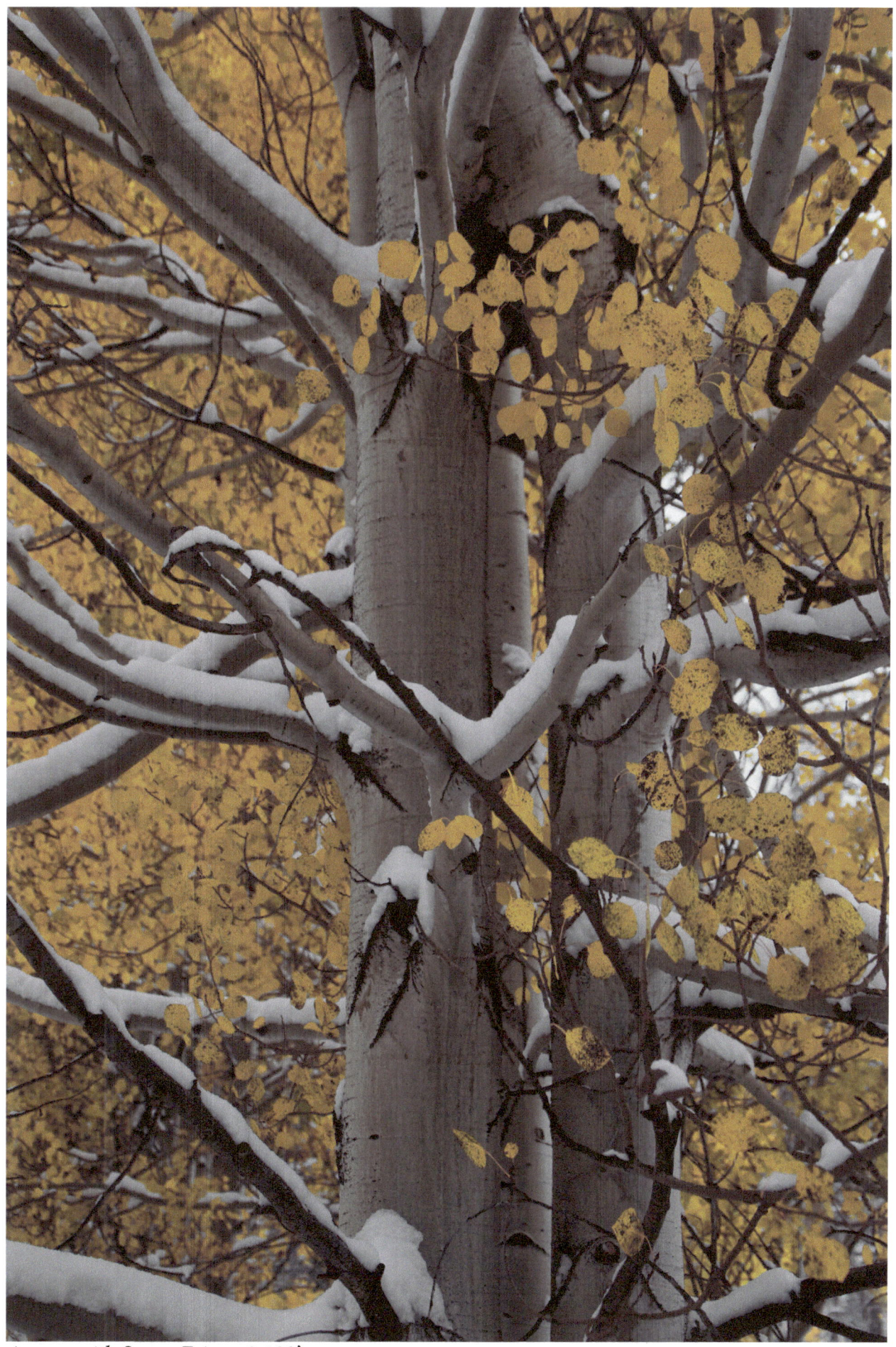

Aspens with Snow, Frisco, 9,120'

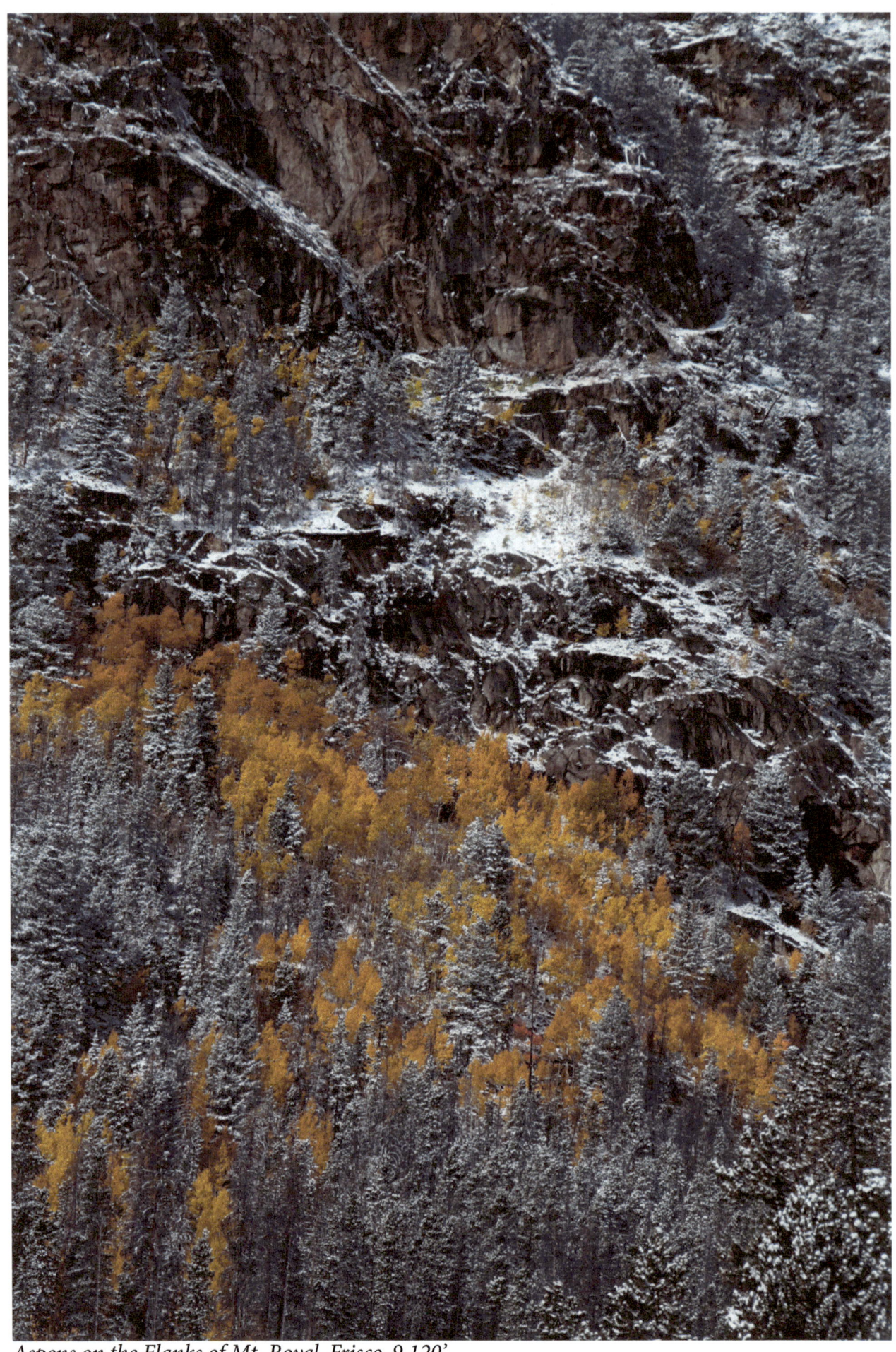

Aspens on the Flanks of Mt. Royal, Frisco, 9,120'

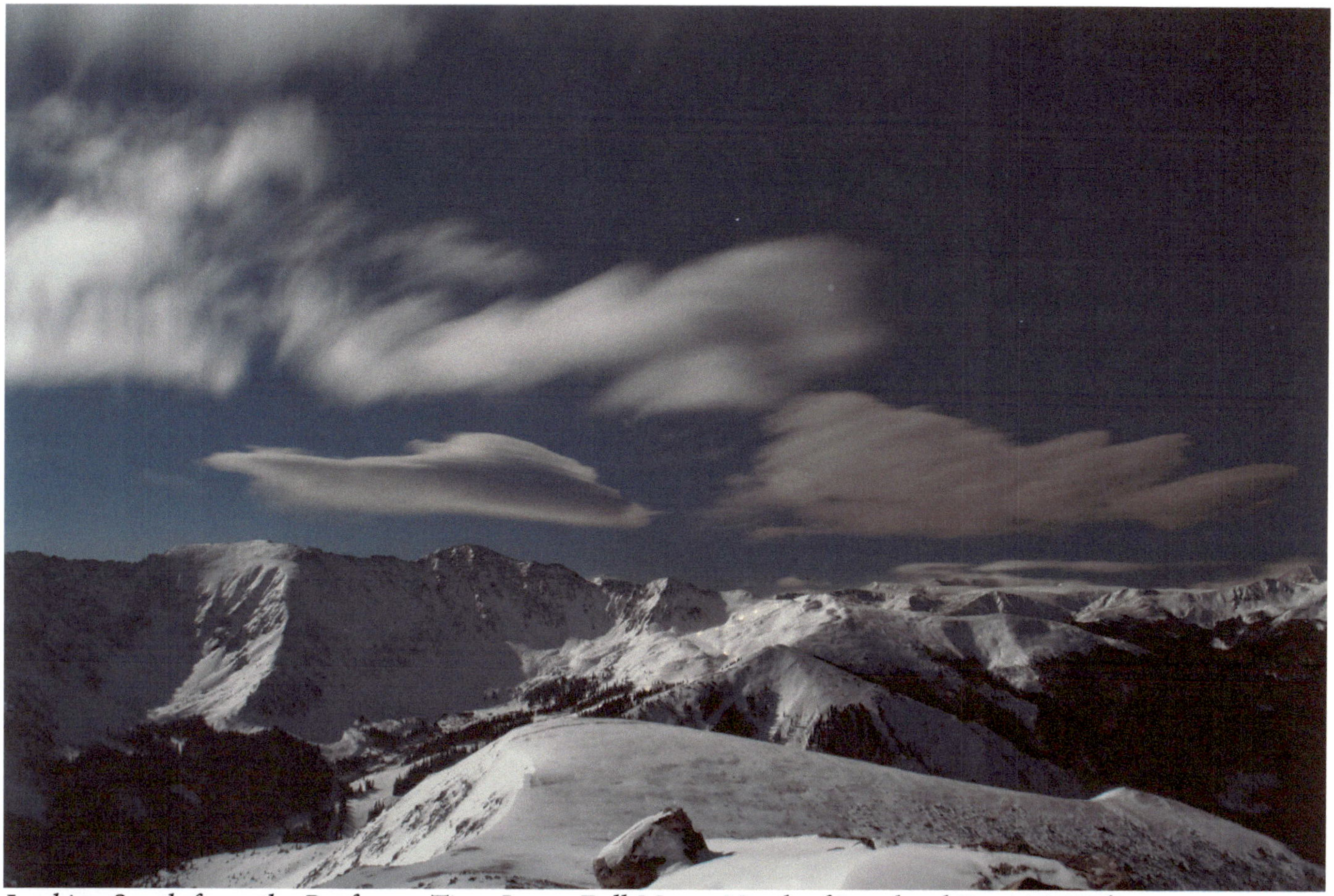

Looking South from the Professor, Time Lapse Full Moon, North of Loveland Pass, 12,470'

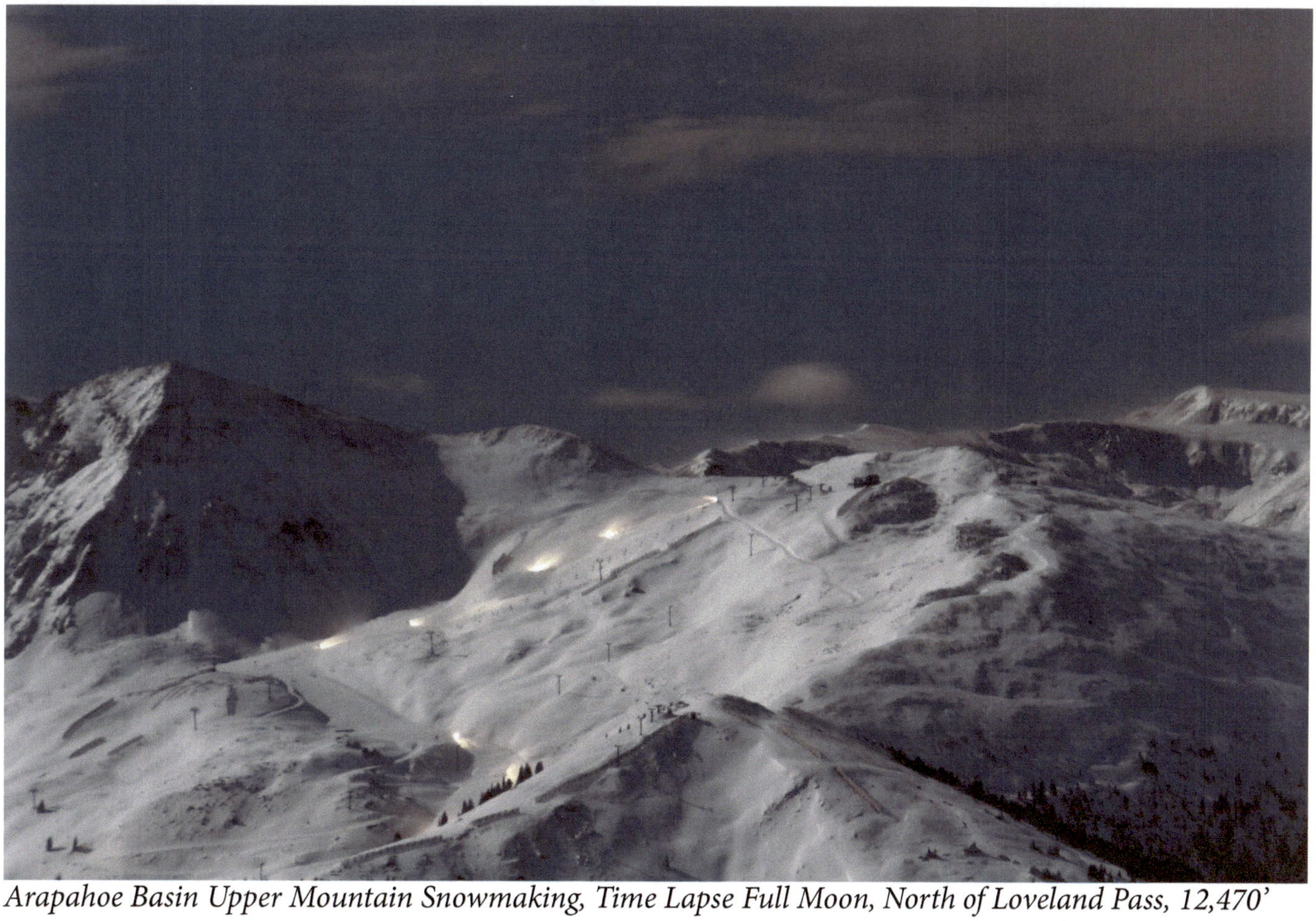

Arapahoe Basin Upper Mountain Snowmaking, Time Lapse Full Moon, North of Loveland Pass, 12,470'

(Prior Pages) Fall comes to an end in the Rockies with an abruptness that seems unnatural. Early in one week, aspens are at their peak. At the end of that same week, it's over. The leaves have fallen, the color is gone, and winter is knocking at the door.

In most places where leaves change, there is an extended period of time between the last leaf that falls and the onset of winter. That transition period is usually longer than the color season itself. In the Rockies, that period lasts, at most, two weeks. The photo on page 72 was taken October 6. The photos on page 73 were taken October 19. In the span of two weeks, the final display of leaves gave way to ski season! Mind you, Arapahoe Basin is at a much higher altitude than where aspen trees grow; however, the existence of the ski area within the same county makes it certainly feel like the transition was that short on a mass scale.

In these two photos on the prior page, it is a full moon and the sun has set. A time-lapse photo is necessary to gather sufficient light to create an image; thus, the clouds have indications of motion and distant peaks show blowing snow. The trek to get the photo was very interesting. Parking at 11,998' at Loveland Pass, the route to the photo site is a 500' elevation gain traversing the continental divide. In all seriousness, it is a steep hill when compared to other climbing options. At that high of an elevation and with 12" of snow on the ground, there is no need for a headlamp as the moon is so bright. The challenge is to find and stay on the trail – and where that is not possible due to waist deep snow drifts, avoiding a twisted ankle is the key as there are extensive piles of alpine rocks to traverse.

The hike consisted of some occasional wind gusts with crisp night air at 11 degrees F. At the summit, the experience can only be described as "spiritual" – standing atop a mountain at 12,500' elevation – with a few counties in view, bright full moon, incredible stars, and a howling wind. There is nothing like it.

As is typical in Colorado, the wind is moody – and it started to blow with a ferocity that I did not expect. Visibility dropped to near zero so it was time to leave. The winds accompanied the entire hike down and required a hike by memory to get back to the parking lot. Fortunately, this was a route I have done many times.

The close-up photo shows snowmaking operations at upper mountain Arapahoe Basin. Snow guns have a small light on them; thus, it looks as though lanterns were placed on the hill.

(Following Pages) The succeeding pages of black and white photos show a unique demonstration of fall. "Black and white, for fall colors?" you might say. Indeed fall is typically something where color is highlighted. Nonetheless, it is a time of impressive contrast in the Rockies. White snow, yellow leaves, dark blue sky, chiseled composition from terrain. Red filter black and white removes color while accentuating contrast and composition, allowing us to see autumn differently.

One of the greatest photographers history has ever known, Ansel Adams, reached fame photographing the American West in black and white. He, of course, was pushed into the artistic genre by virtue of film technology limitations. However, his work – and that of many great photographers of the era – was a practice of greater difficulty requiring the artist to present composition and angle while redacting the initial pizazz of color. Much like many things of his time, those who mastered challenging skills early in the mechanical technology era had an exquisite talent and presentation that is unmatched. While computerized technology has opened many fields of activity to the masses, simplicity occludes refined craftsmanship that was learned by the greatest artists in times past. Masterful black and white photography is to be savored by connoisseurs of the art who have developed an appreciation for fine taste required to deliver the unconventional.

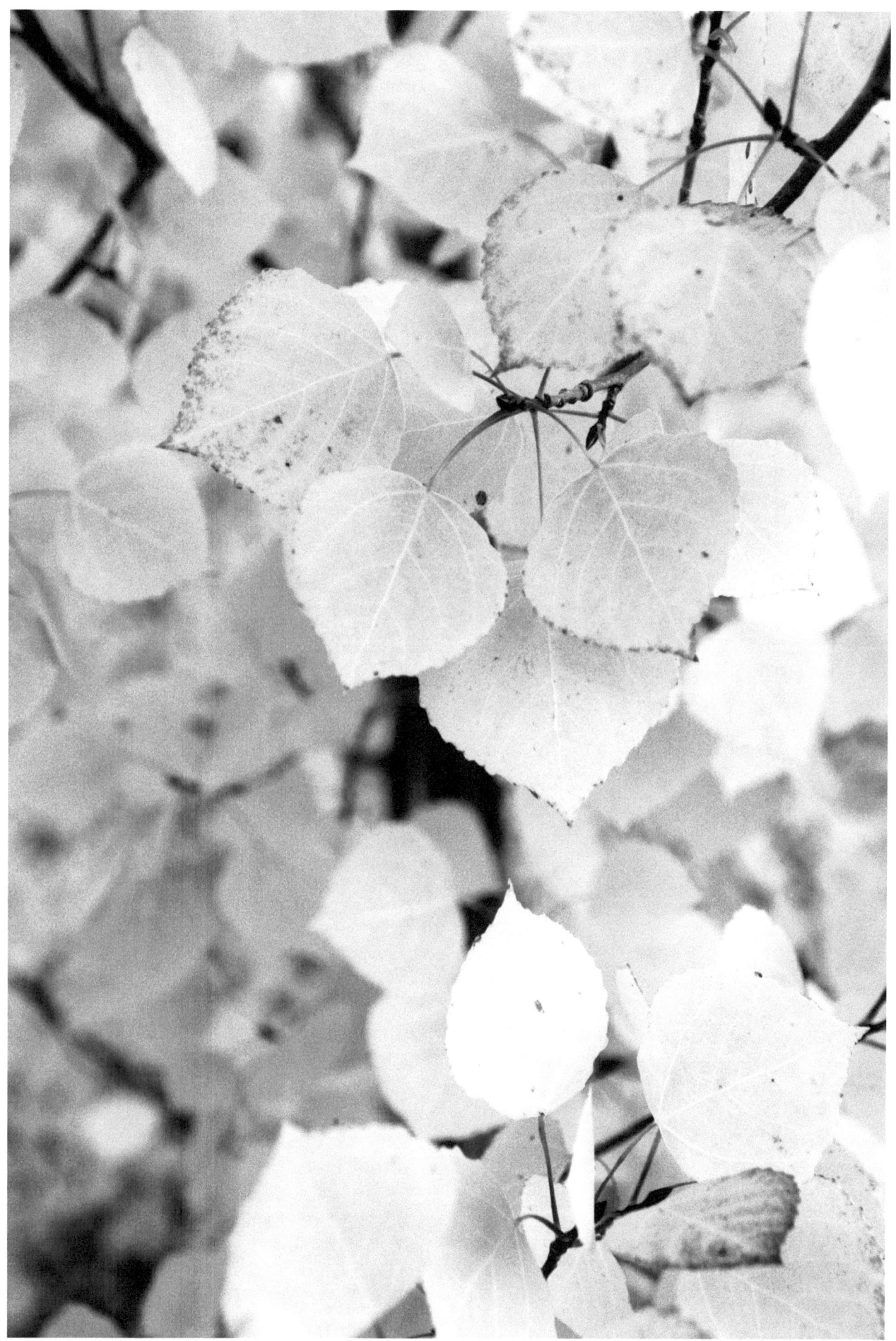

Aspen Leaves, Base of Mt. Royal, Frisco, 9,160'

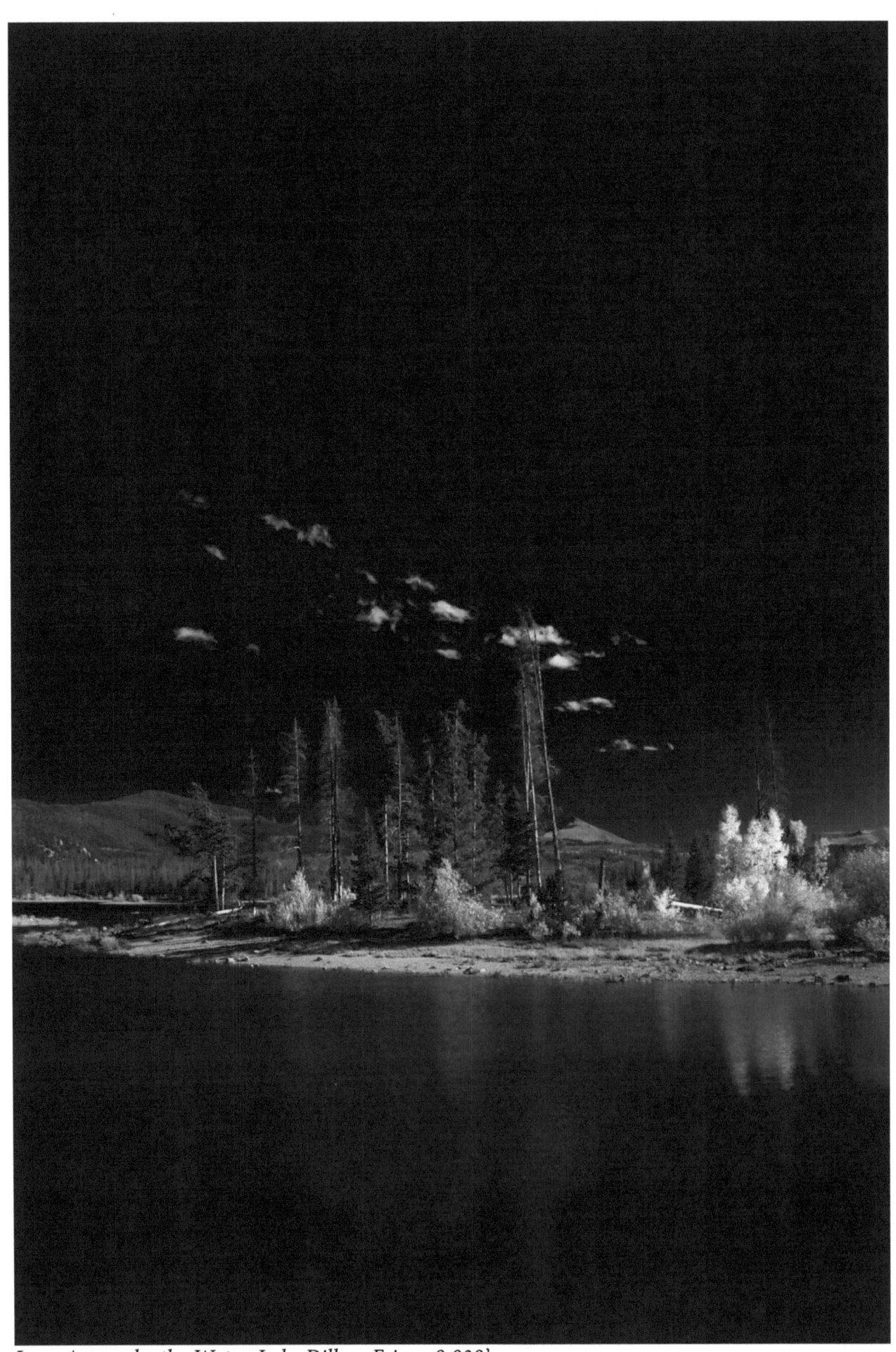

Lone Aspens by the Water, Lake Dillon, Frisco, 9,030'

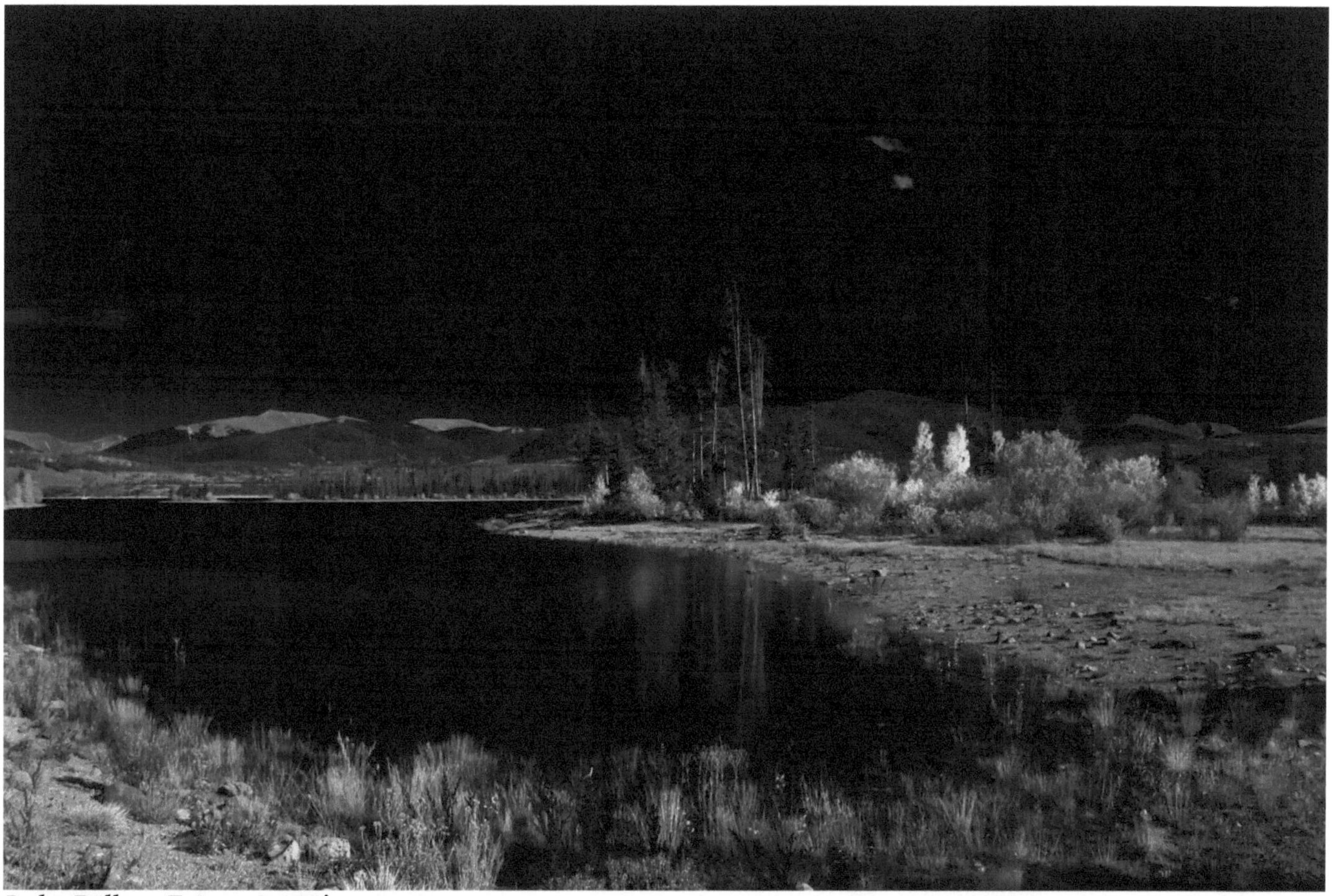

Lake Dillon, Frisco, 9,030'

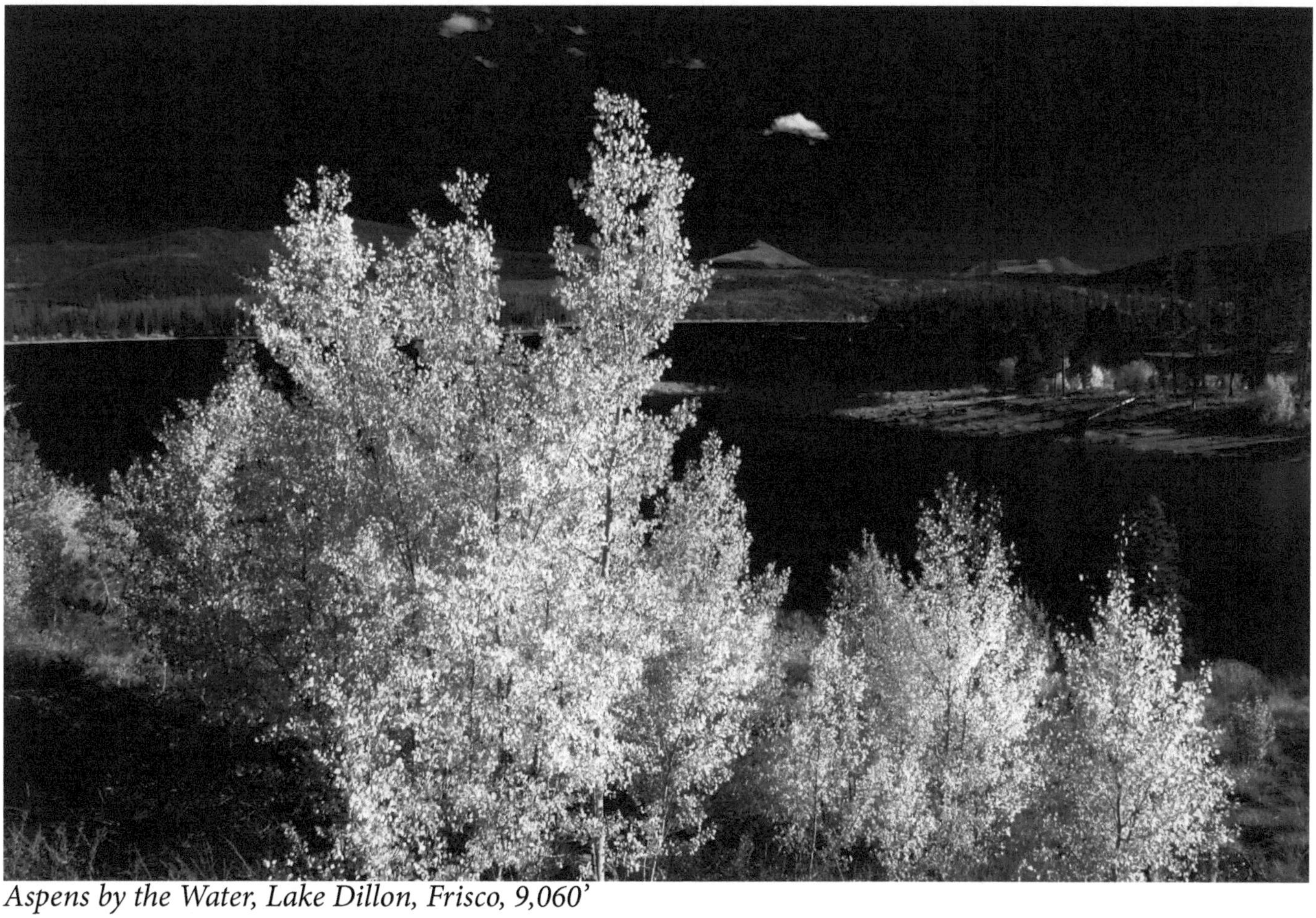

Aspens by the Water, Lake Dillon, Frisco, 9,060'

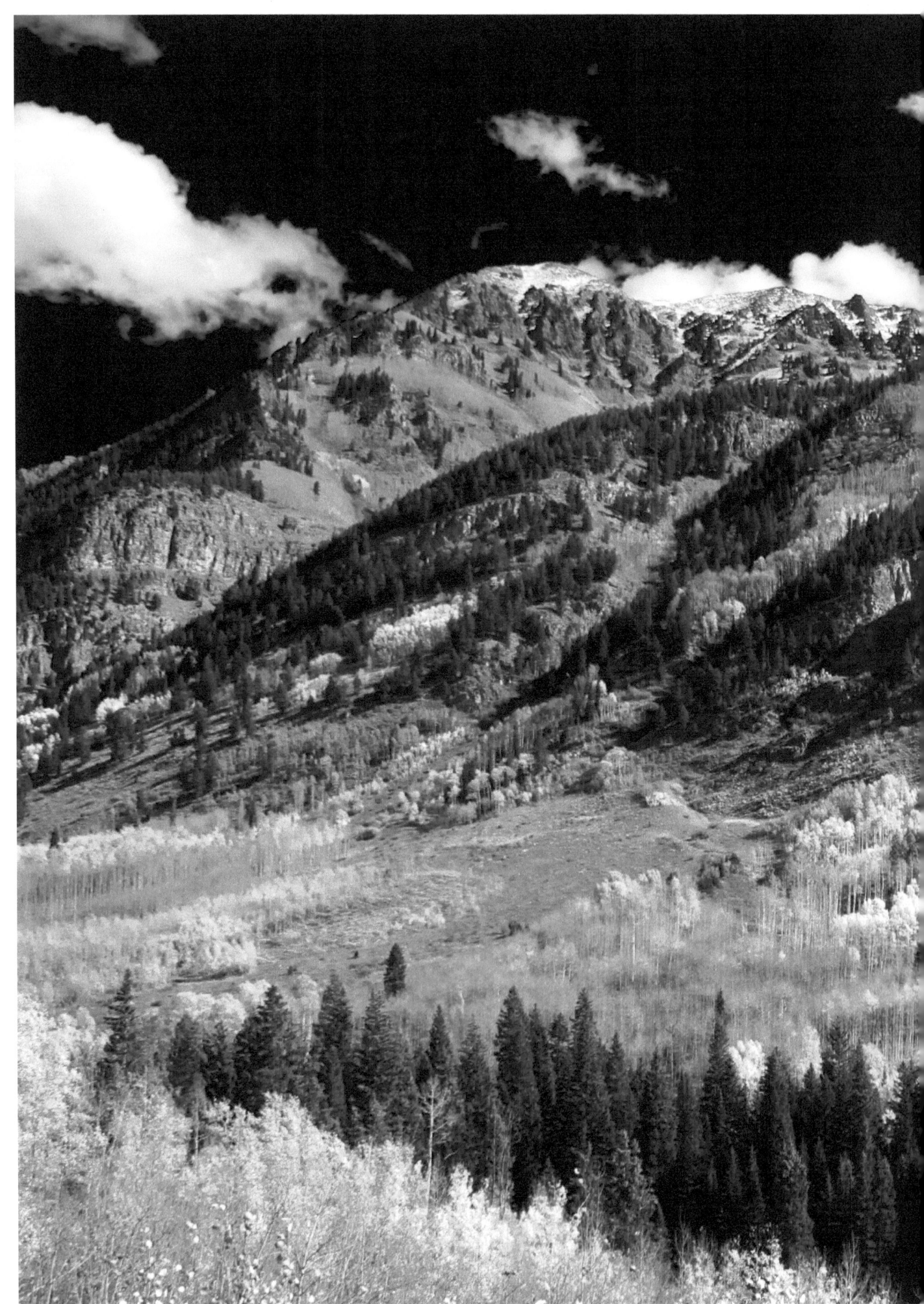

Maroon Creek Rd, Aspen, 8,820'

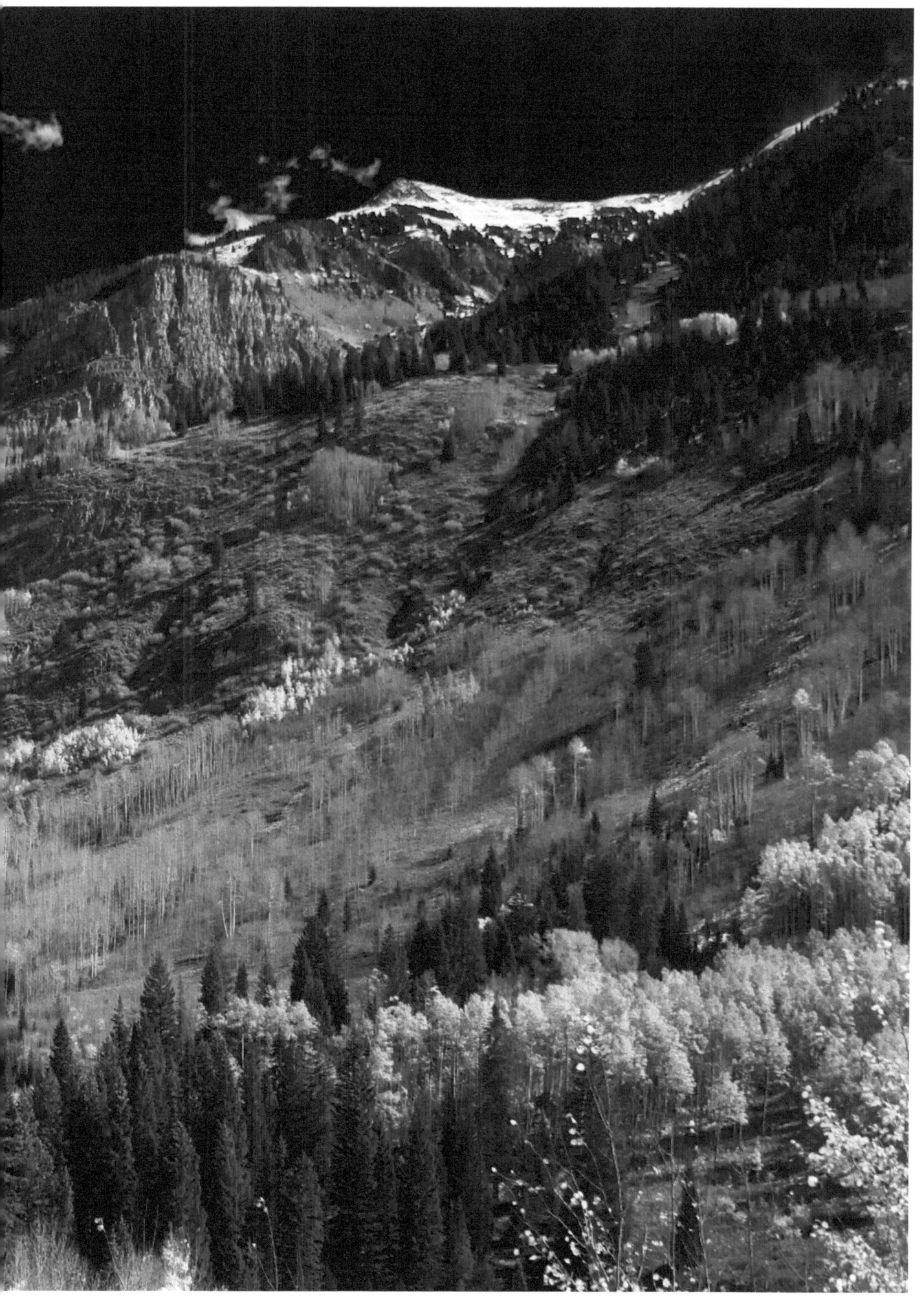

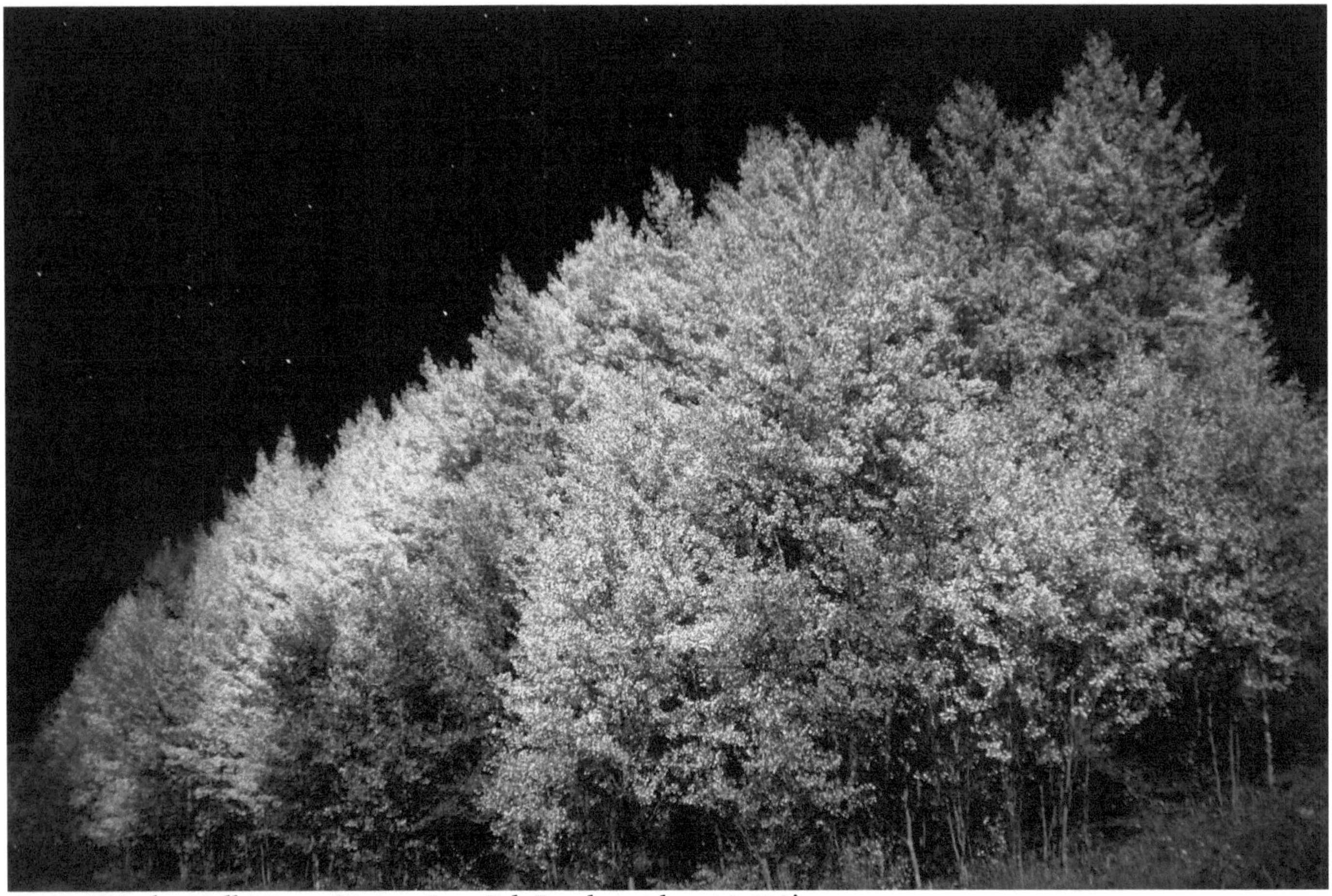

Aspens Under Full Moon, Boreas Pass Rd, Breckenridge, 10,630'

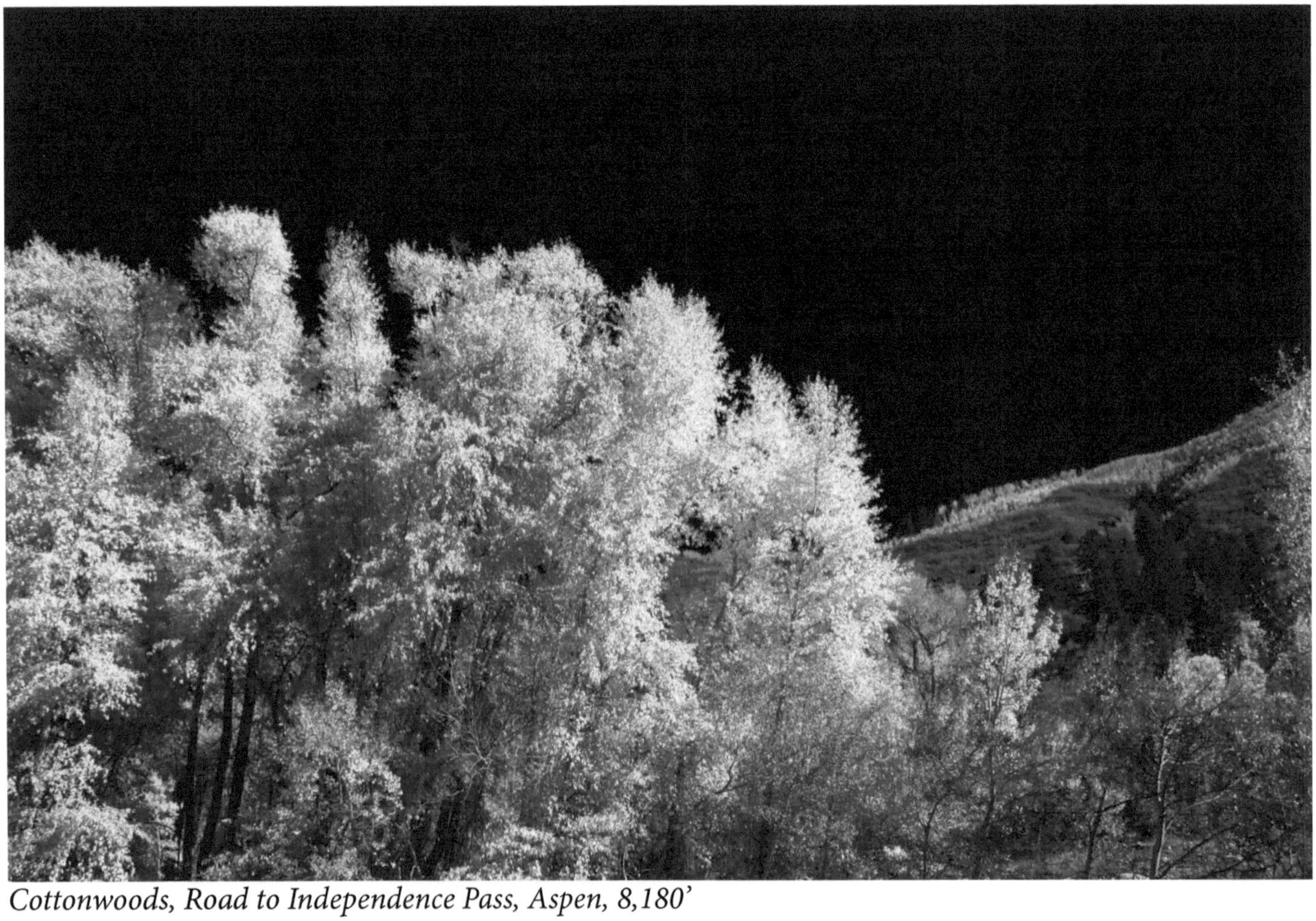

Cottonwoods, Road to Independence Pass, Aspen, 8,180'

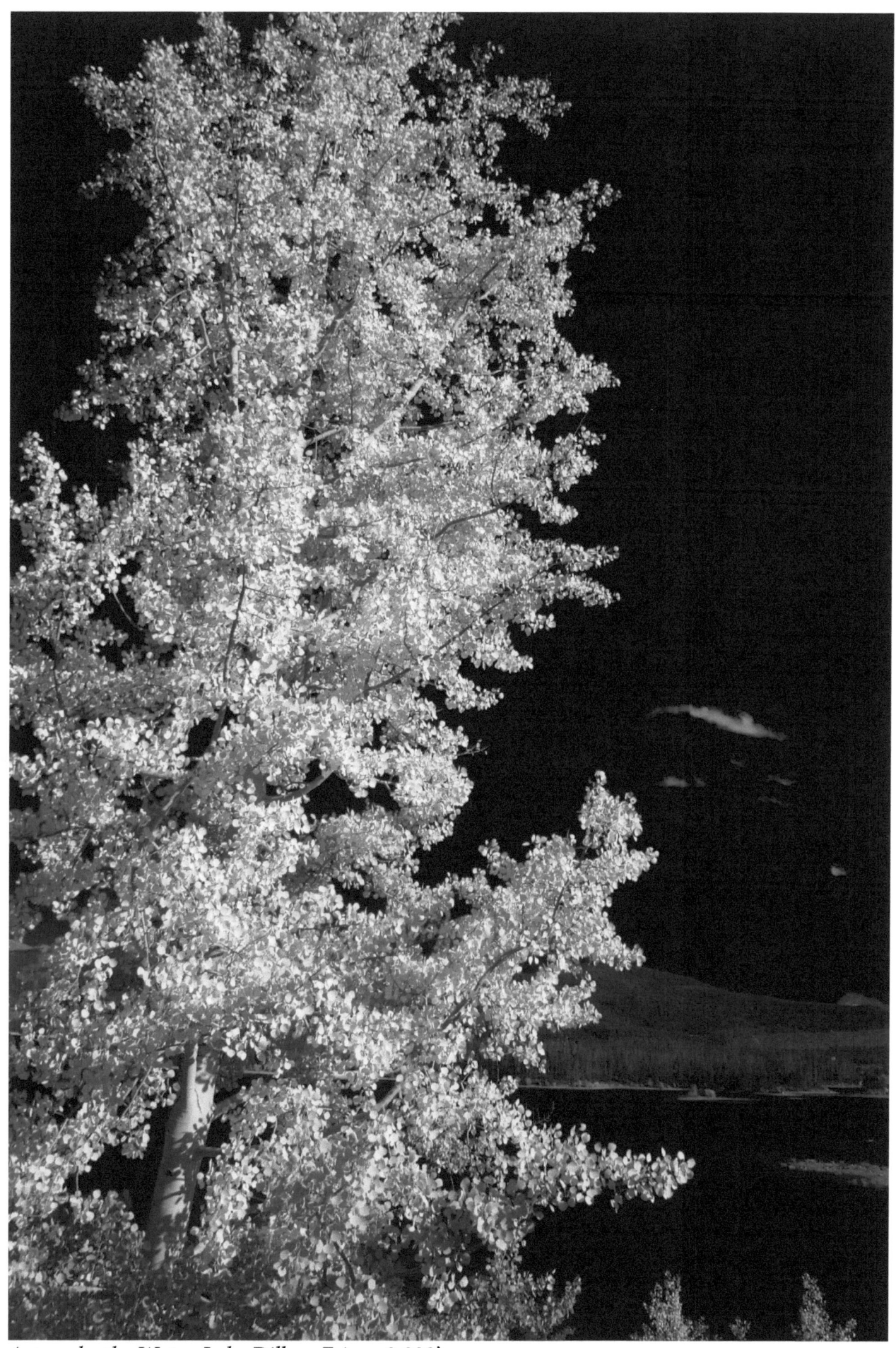

Aspens by the Water, Lake Dillon, Frisco, 9,080'

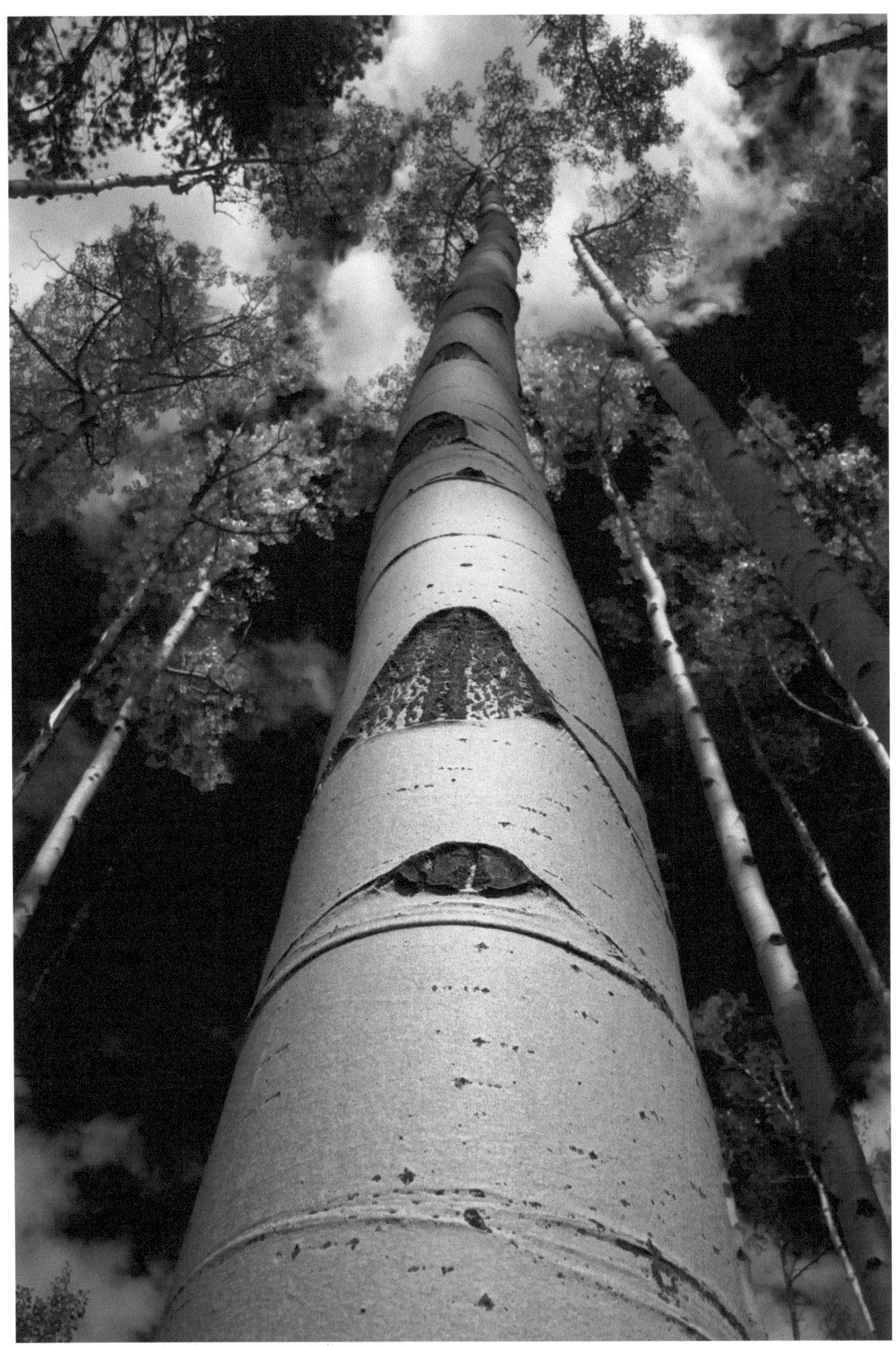

Aspen, Miners Creek, Frisco, 9,120'

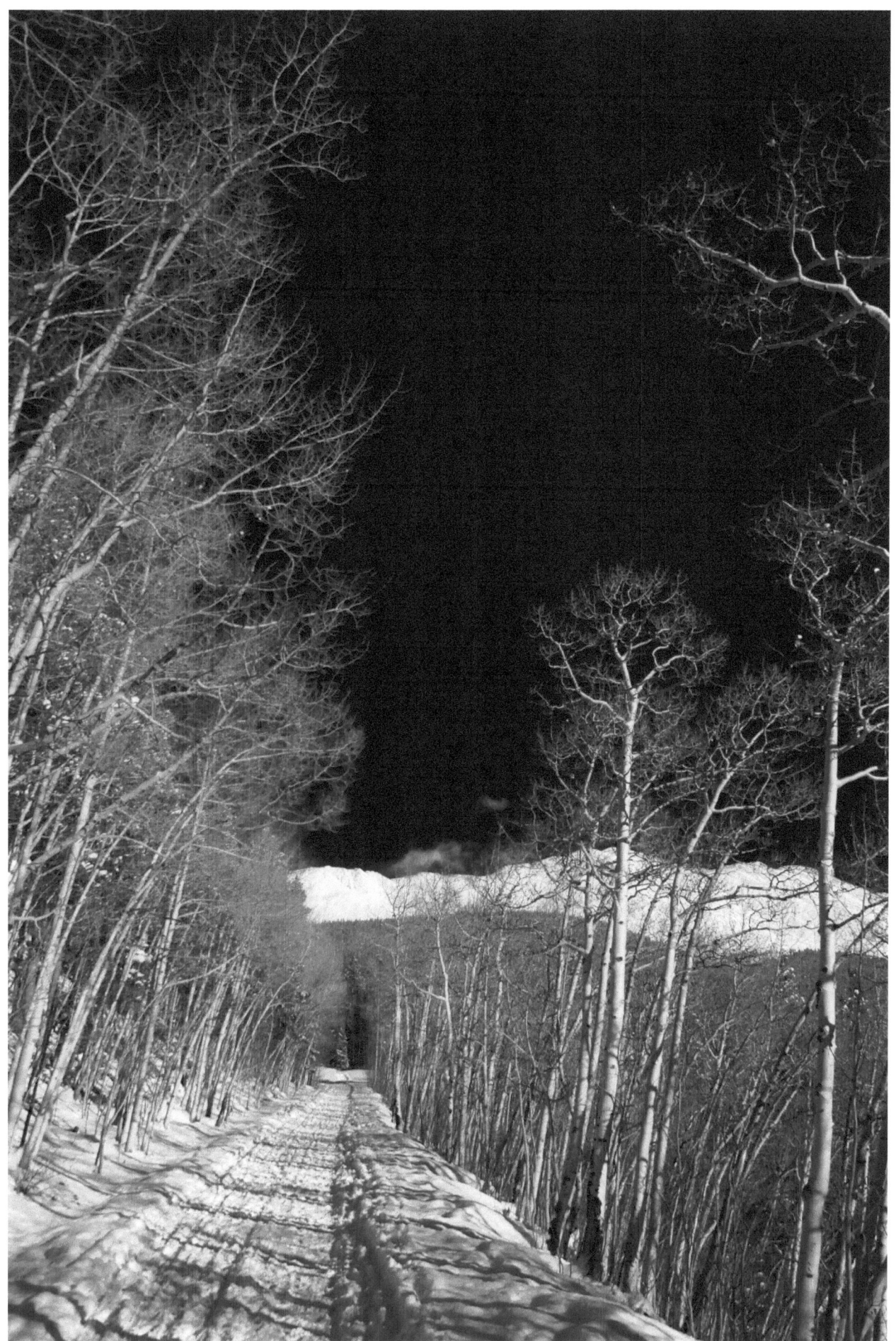

Aspens in Winter, Boreas Pass Rd - Breckenridge, 10,470'

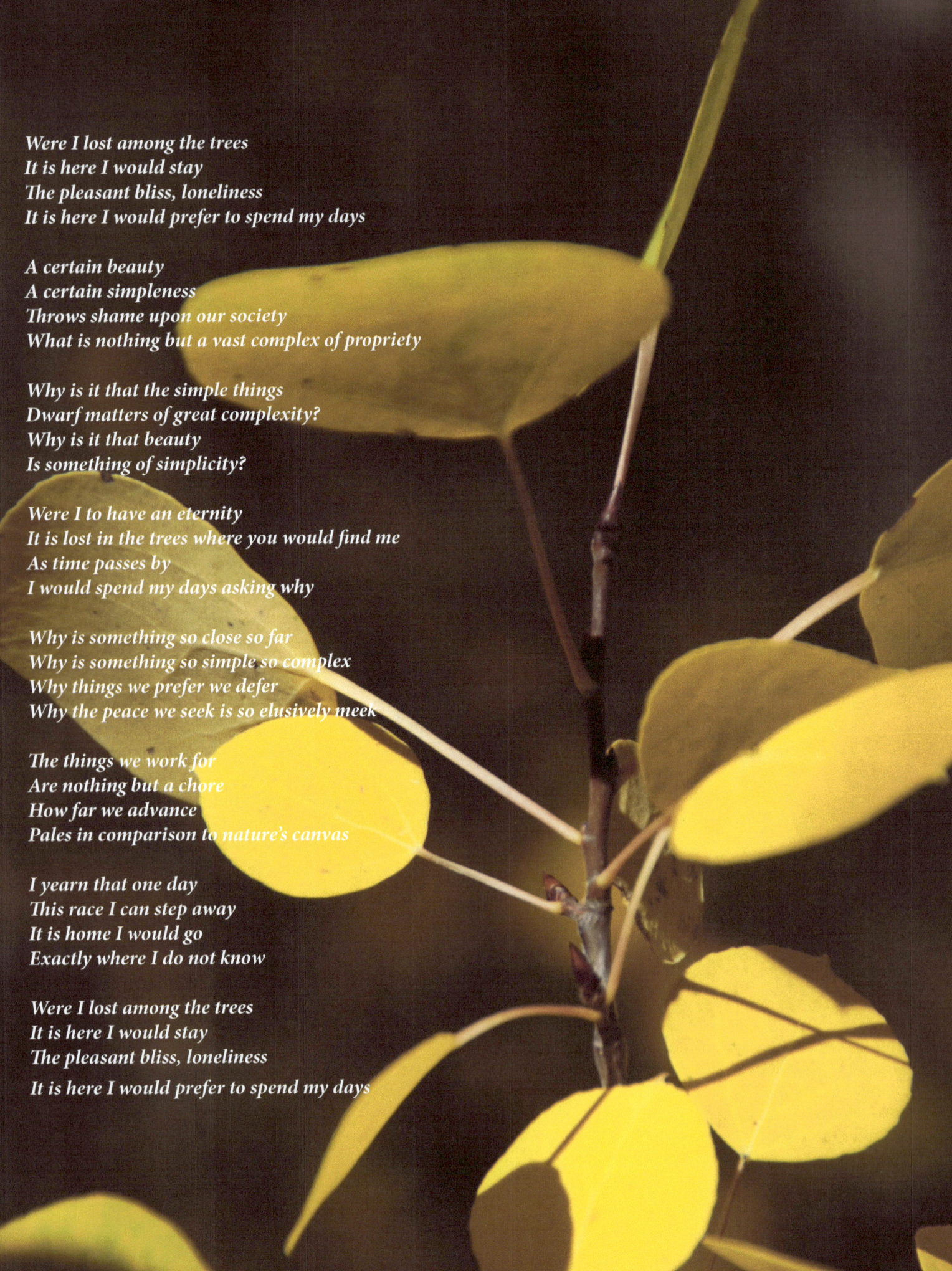

Were I lost among the trees
It is here I would stay
The pleasant bliss, loneliness
It is here I would prefer to spend my days

A certain beauty
A certain simpleness
Throws shame upon our society
What is nothing but a vast complex of propriety

Why is it that the simple things
Dwarf matters of great complexity?
Why is it that beauty
Is something of simplicity?

Were I to have an eternity
It is lost in the trees where you would find me
As time passes by
I would spend my days asking why

Why is something so close so far
Why is something so simple so complex
Why things we prefer we defer
Why the peace we seek is so elusively meek

The things we work for
Are nothing but a chore
How far we advance
Pales in comparison to nature's canvas

I yearn that one day
This race I can step away
It is home I would go
Exactly where I do not know

Were I lost among the trees
It is here I would stay
The pleasant bliss, loneliness
It is here I would prefer to spend my days